IMAGES
of Rail

SOUTHERN PACIFIC'S SLIM PRINCESS

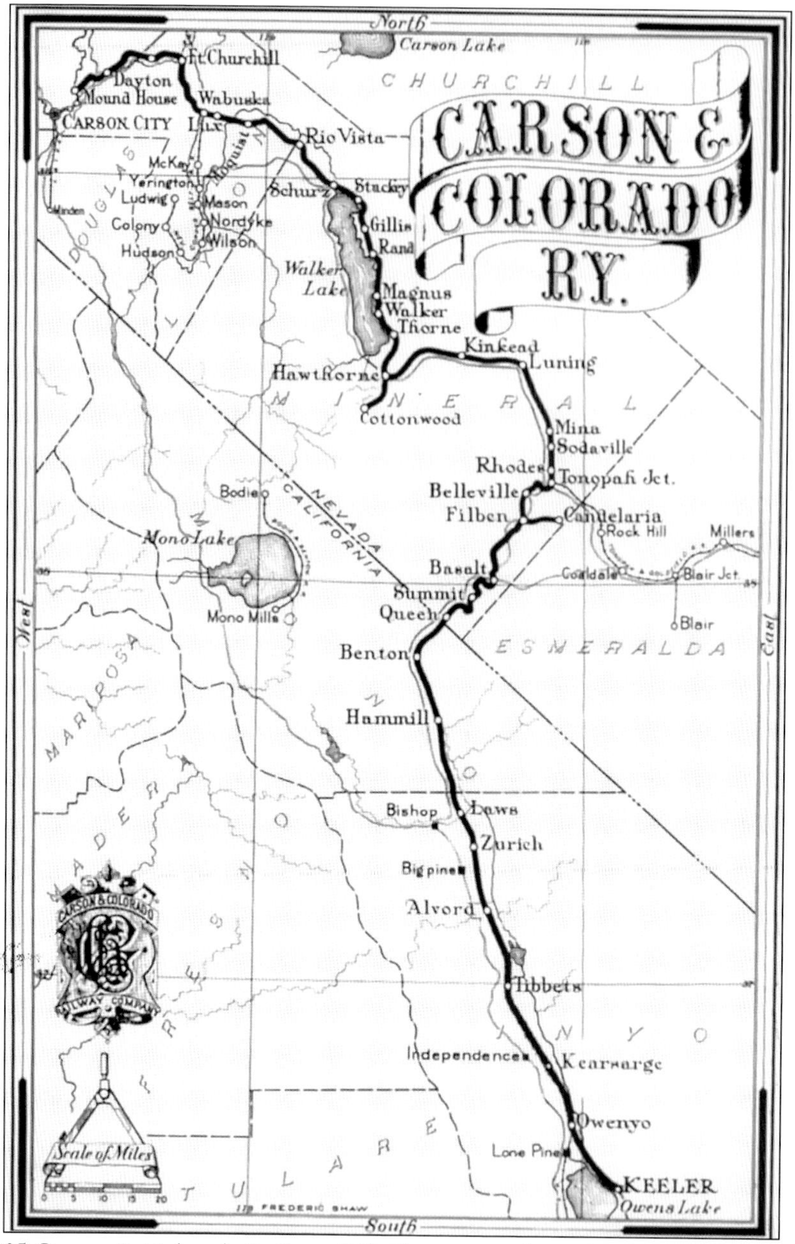

This c. 1905 Carson & Colorado Railway (C&C) map was drawn by Capt. Frederic J. Shaw in 1949. This map gives an overview of the entire 300-mile railroad from Mound House to Keeler. Also shown are two branch lines constructed by the C&C. The Cottonwood Branch was built from Hawthorne to Cottonwood to a cordwood loading camp to fuel costs. The Candelaria Branch from Filbin to Candelaria served the town of Candelaria and the mines on Candelaria Mountain. (Author's collection.)

On the Cover: A westbound train led by locomotive No. 18 takes on water at the Kearsarge tank while the crew poses in a candid moment. The crew members seen in this photograph are, from left to right, engineer Walter C. "Fergie" Ferguson, conductor Jim Brennan, and brakemen Bob Olson and Jerry Jones. (Photograph by Charles Ward; courtesy of the Stephen E. Drew collection.)

IMAGES
of Rail

SOUTHERN PACIFIC'S SLIM PRINCESS

Andrew Brandon

ARCADIA
PUBLISHING

ISBN 978-1-4671-0878-2

Published by Arcadia Publishing
Charleston, South Carolina

Printed in the United States of America

Library of Congress Control Number: 2022936848

For all general information, please contact Arcadia Publishing:
Telephone 843-853-2070
Fax 843-853-0044
E-mail sales@arcadiapublishing.com
For customer service and orders:
Toll-Free 1-888-313-2665

Visit us on the Internet at www.arcadiapublishing.com

This book is dedicated to the men and women who brought the Slim Princess to life and those who continue to preserve its memory.

Contents

ACKNOWLEDGMENTS

The creation of this book would not have been possible without the assistance of several individuals and organizations. I am extremely grateful to fellow author and historian Stephen E. Drew for allowing the use of photographs and ephemera from his personal collection. Additionally, I want to thank Herman Darr, Martin E. Hansen, Larry Jensen, Dennis Burke, Brian Norden, John Friend, Randy Hees, Kyle Wyatt, Taylor Rush, Prof. Fred Matthews, and the Southern Pacific Narrow Gauge Historical Society for providing additional photographs and historical research. Jared Woldseth, Herman Darr, and Brian Norden provided proofreading editorial advice on the text through the final stages of the project. I would also like to thank my editor with Arcadia Publishing, Caroline (Anderson) Vickerson for her patience and assistance throughout the course of writing this book.

Several museums provided access to photograph surviving equipment from the railroad for this project: Travel Town Railroad Museum in Griffith Park, Los Angeles; Southern California Railway Museum in Perris, California; California State Railroad Museum in Sacramento, California; Nevada County Narrow Gauge Railroad Museum in Nevada City, California; Nevada State Railroad Museum in Carson City, Nevada; and Laws Historical Site and Railroad Museum in Laws, California.

The late Richard C. Datin Jr. took a number of photographs of the railroad during the last few years of operation, many of which have been used in this book. I am fortunate to have these negatives and photographic prints in my collection, and he has been given credit for them accordingly. Unless otherwise noted, all images and documents are from the author's personal collection.

Finally, this project would not have been possible without the patience and support of my wife, Elizabeth. Her assistance in proofreading the text and asking questions regarding railroad terminology was invaluable.

INTRODUCTION

Few narrow-gauge railroads in the West have been romanticized like the Carson & Colorado Railway. Since 1869, the directors of the Virginia & Truckee Railroad (V&T) made a substantial business of transporting silver ore by railroad to mills along the Carson River. The railroad was born from the wealth of the famed Comstock Lode around Virginia City, Nevada. In the late 1870s, the V&T took an interest in the developing mining camps at Aurora, Bodie, and Candelaria. A survey was made for a route toward these camps, as the railroad's financiers sought the next big mining boom over the southern horizon. By 1880, output on the Comstock was declining and the plan to extend the V&T south changed. A narrow-gauge affiliate known as the Carson & Colorado Railway was established. The new railroad was projected to stretch between the Carson River in Nevada and the Colorado River in California, near the Arizona border. Within three years, construction crews had built 300 miles of railroad connecting Mound House, Nevada, with Keeler, California. For nearly 80 years, the railroad was the only transportation system through the deserts and rugged mountains of western Nevada and eastern California.

Revenue on the C&C never met expectations, and the railroad was not as profitable as had been hoped. The mining boom in Candelaria ended shortly after the railroad arrived and the shipment of silver ore over the railroad ended. By the 1890s, passenger traffic was intermittent, and freight traffic was largely agricultural. Plans to extend the line south out of Keeler were halted. At the end of the 19th century, the railroad was operating at a loss and its owners sought relief from the financial burden. In March 1900, they sold the railroad to Collis P. Huntington's Southern Pacific Company (SP). The C&C never lived up to expectations, and the directors were glad to be rid of the railroad and recover $2.75 million from SP. Just over that horizon, however, was the next big boom. Discoveries of silver and gold at Tonopah in 1900, followed by Goldfield in 1902, brought business beyond SP's dreams shortly after it acquired the line. The railroad was the closest connection to the strike and became an important lifeline to the region.

The Tonopah boom revived the railroad, and SP began upgrading the line to meet the new traffic demands. The northern portion of the railroad, nearly 150 miles of the railroad from Mound House to Tonopah Junction, was converted to standard gauge. A new railroad yard to transfer freight from the standard-gauge to narrow-gauge cars was established at Mina. The new town of Mina was established by the railroad to house employees and built expansive railroad facilities. The southern portion from Mina, Nevada, south to Keeler, California, remained narrow gauge and became known as the SP's Mina Branch. For the next 55 years of Southern Pacific ownership, the railroad brought commerce and development to a rural landscape. Commodities hauled by the railroad included perlite, soda ash, pumice, dolomite, talc, tungsten, and even livestock. In 1909, SP completed the final leg of the Jawbone Branch from Mojave to Owenyo, fulfilling the dream that went unrealized by the railroad's founders. It was the Southern Pacific that provided the former C&C with the nickname "Slim Princess," a nickname still intertwined with the history of the railroad.

Rumors persisted about SP planning to convert the remaining narrow gauge from Mina to Keeler over to standard gauge. When the Tonopah boom slowed during the 1920s, the hope of converting it dried up as traffic over the narrow gauge began to decline. Just prior to the start of World War II, the narrow gauge from Mina to Laws was removed. The remaining line from Laws to Keeler became the SP's Keeler Branch. The Keeler Branch was the last operating common carrier narrow-gauge railroad in Nevada and California. The railroad was adored by aficionados, called railfans, who organized fan trips over the railroad during the final years. Hollywood found the Owens Valley and neighboring Alabama Hills as a region that captured the imagination. The desert landscape bordered by the Sierra Nevada range and Mount Whitney, the tallest peak in California, to the north created the perfect backdrop for the west. The Slim Princess starred in several films due to its close proximity to the Alabama Hills, a popular filming location for serial westerns. The end came in April 1960 when the Interstate Commerce Commission allowed SP to abandon service.

The Slim Princess is celebrated in folklore; it formed an important link with the regions it served. Memories and tributes to the railroad linger through the regions it served, and remains of the railroad can still be found along the route. Foundations, grades, and stonework are still visible along the route. Equipment used on the line is preserved at multiple museums throughout Nevada and California. Portions of the original C&C remain in use by the Union Pacific Railroad and US Army from Churchill to Thorne. In the Owens Valley, the yard at Laws was donated to Inyo County and remains as a tribute to the days when the railroad was still the important link to the outside world. At the southern terminal of the railroad at Keeler, the depot and structures of the yard facility along with former industries stand silently, ghosts of an area that once generated substantial revenue for the railroad.

This book is intended to provide a concise overview of the Southern Pacific's narrow gauge from 1912 until its demise in 1960. The history of the SP narrow gauge is too complex to be told in a single volume, and many stations were excluded from this book. Important stations like the terminal at Mina, Montgomery Pass, Benton, Hammil, Laws, Aberdeen, Kearsarge, Owenyo, and Keeler make up the focus. Whenever possible, the most accurate information on the history of the railroad and equipment has been used in photograph captions at the time of this writing. Readers interested in learning more about the railroad are encouraged to look deeper into the sources listed in the bibliography. For the period focused on in this book, *Southern Pacific's Slim Princess in the Sunset 1940–1960* by Joe Dale Morris and *Southern Pacific Narrow Gauge Locomotives and Freight Equipment* by Robert Bader are essential resources.

Finally, it is important to note Southern Pacific's parlance that will be used in this book. With thousands of miles of track to manage, SP standardized its terminology across the railroad. Captions in this book use SP's terminology when describing the movement of trains. Trains that are headed toward San Francisco, the location of SP's headquarters, are considered "westbound," and trains headed away from San Francisco were considered "eastbound." These directions are used independently of geographic direction. On the Slim Princess, this meant a train headed to Keeler, on the southern end of the line, was "eastbound" and to Mina, Nevada, on the northern end, was a "westbound" train. Additionally, SP maintained a difference in terminology between a station and a depot. A station was a point or location on the railroad. A depot is a building located at a station. This meant named sidings or yards were stations, even those without depots.

One

Carson & Colorado Railroad

As the fabled Comstock boom started to wane, the investors of the Virginia & Truckee Railroad took interest in mining discoveries in southern Nevada and eastern California. These remote mining strikes relied on wagon teams to haul ore and supplies. Having prior success in the railroad business, it believed a narrow-gauge railroad would benefit the region. The Carson & Colorado Railroad was incorporated on May 10, 1880. The railroad bore the name of the two rivers it planned to connect: the Carson River near Mound House, Nevada, and the Colorado River near Mojave. Henry M. Yerington, superintendent and vice president of the V&T, served as president of the C&C, with Duane L. Bliss as vice president. Investors of the V&T, Darius Ogden Mills and William Sharon, were the primary stockholders in the C&C.

On May 31, 1880, construction started at Mound House, Nevada. Within a year, the railroad stretched 100 miles, reaching Hawthorne at the south end of Walker Lake on April 7, 1881. The railroad auctioned off lots for the townsite and constructed engine facilities and passenger and freight depots. The mining camps of Belleville and Candelaria were reached shortly thereafter. By the time the railroad arrived, the mining activity began to decline and the expected freight traffic never materialized.

Undaunted, the railroad continued building south toward Owens Valley and the mining camps of Benton, Cerro Gordo, and Darwin by way of Montgomery Pass. The route over Montgomery Pass was built to a maximum 2.33 percent grade and featured the only tunnel on the line as it descended to the valley floor. The railroad reached Bishop Creek and established a station. In mid-March 1883, Bishop Creek was renamed Laws. In July, track reached the eastern shore of Owens Lake and the community of Keeler.

The railroad turned a meager profit, and plans for expansion to the Colorado River were shelved in the late 1880s. In February 1892, the railroad was reorganized as the Carson & Colorado Railway. For the next eight years, it turned a small profit, but those earnings were not enough to satisfy the investors who sought to rid themselves of the financial burden. In late 1899 and early 1900, D.O. Mills negotiated with C.P. Huntington of the Southern Pacific for the sale of the C&C to the Southern Pacific Company. The transfer of ownership occurred on March 1, 1900.

Construction of the Carson & Colorado Railroad began at Mound House in 1881. At that time, it was a small station on the Virginia & Truckee Railroad. To accommodate the new narrow-gauge railroad, a larger depot was constructed that served both railroads. These two views show the Virginia & Truckee side (above) and the Carson & Colorado side (below).

Dayton was the first station after Mound House. The V&T moved the original Mound House depot here in 1880 and constructed a new building to serve the interchange. Located along the Carson River, the community of Dayton was the location of several ore mills and the famed Sutro Tunnel. The C&C served the town with a yard and a branch to the Rock Point Mill, located on the eastern side of town. (Courtesy of the Stephen E. Drew collection.)

Between Mound House and Dayton, the railroad encountered the steepest part of the railroad as the grade descended into the Dayton Valley. Once the grade entered the valley, it leveled as it continued through the valley to the station. In this photograph, a train can be seen approaching Dayton from the west. Boxcar No. 306, seen at right, was a metal-sheathed car from the LaMothe Manufacturing Company. (Courtesy of the Stephen E. Drew collection.)

After following the Carson River for 20 miles, the railroad turned south and was constructed into the Mason valley. North of the existing settlement of Pizen Switch, the railroad was established at the station at Wabuska. In this photograph, locomotive No. 3 and train pause in Wabuska before continuing east to Walker Lake and Hawthorne.

A NEW RAILROAD.

Carson and Colorado Railroad,
Nevada.
NOW IN OPERATION TO HAWTHORNE
110 MILES SOUTH OF CARSON, NEV.

The direct, shortest and cheapest route for freight and passengers to the following mining towns and camps: Aurora, Bodie, Bridgeport, Belleville, Candelaria, Columbus, Benton, Montezuma, Silver Peak, Alida Valley, Bishop Creek and Gold Mountain.

C. and C. R. R. trains make close connection at Mound House Station with trains of Virginia and Truckee Railroad, making close connection at Reno with East and West bound trains of the C. P. R. R.

Passengers leaving San Francisco and Sacramento on C P. Overland train arrive at Hawthorne and connect with U. S. Stage Company's line of Concord coaches at 2:45 P. M. of the following day, arriving at Bodie same evening.

Wells, Fargo & Co.'s line of Fast Freight Wagons leave Hawthorne daily, delivering fast freight in Bodie within 36 hours from San Francisco.

To insure dispatch by team transportation from Hawthorne, shippers are requested to mark freight Care D. W. Earle & Co., Forwarders, Hawthorne, Nev.

General Office, Carson, Nev.

H M YERINGTON, Gen'l Supt. D. A. BENDER. Gen'l Freight & Pass. Agent.

The railroad reached Hawthorne, Nevada, on April 18, 1881. A townsite was mapped by the railroad and lots sold at an auction. The railroad established passenger and freight depots along with a shop complex for maintaining locomotives. Hawthorne's location provided passengers with stage connections to various mining camps in the region.

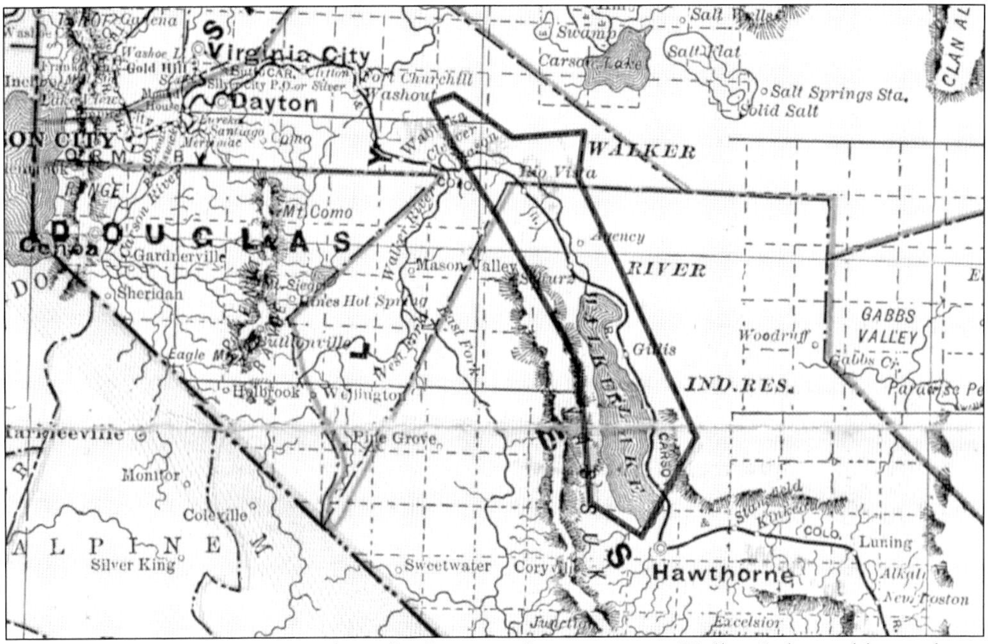

As the railroad was constructed south, the most direct route to Walker Lake and beyond was through the Walker River Paiute tribe's reservation. In 1880, the railroad reached an agreement with the tribe, paying them $750 and allowing free transportation on the railroad for tribe members, along with fish and other goods. The Carson & Colorado passed through the reservation from the northwest down to Walker Lake, where it followed the eastern shoreline down to Hawthorne. This image was published by the George F. Cram Company in 1888.

The agreement with the railroad did not provide members of the tribe with the privilege of riding inside the passenger cars. Instead, their free accommodation was restricted to riding on the car roofs. Here, a group of Paiutes is seen on top of C&C express car No. 300 leaving Mound House. No. 300 was one of four LaMothe patent boxcars converted to Wells Fargo Express cars. (Photograph by Edwin R Jackson; courtesy of the Kyle Wyatt collection.)

The C&C reached Belleville in December 1881. In this photograph is the C&C spur to the upper Northern Belle mill. The second C&C spur to the lower Northern Belle mill can be seen in the center-right of the photograph. Belleville, which can be seen in the valley below, eventually reached a population of 500. The depot and two water tanks are visible in the distance, along with the wye track where a locomotive is being turned. (Courtesy of the University Nevada Reno Special Collections.)

A conductor holds two empty mailbags between trains at an unknown location along the line. Boxcar No. 307, on the left side of the image, is another of the LaMothe patent "pipe" boxcars. LaMothe cars were designed to use commercial gas pipes to construct their framing. Minimal wood was utilized in their construction, notably the doors and the floor inside. The exterior of the cars was sheathed in metal attached to the gas pipe structure. (Courtesy of the Stephen E. Drew collection.)

The daily mixed train waits alongside the depot in Candelaria during the 1890s. The railroad constructed a depot, yard, turntable, and single-stall enginehouse along the north face of Candelaria Mountain. In 1906, the depot was dismantled due to a lack of traffic over the branch. Mining occurred intermittently during the 20th century, and the Candelaria Branch sat unused after 1915; it was removed in 1932. The crew members are, from left to right, Bill Robinson, engineer; Charles Meadows, mail clerk; Fred Barnes, conductor; John McGillis, fireman; and Frank Regan, brakeman.

Northern Belle Mine was located at the end of the track in Candelaria. Ore from the mine was loaded into four-wheel dump cars and shipped to the mills at Belleville or the Mount Diablo Mill, near Sodaville, for processing. The C&C operated 15 of the little dump cars, which were purchased from the V&T and converted to three-foot gauge. They were sold in 1899 to the Pacific Coast Borax Company and used in California.

The Carson & Colorado traversed hundreds of miles of rugged terrain. During construction, the surveyors encountered few obstacles on the route until Montgomery Pass. The railroad wound up and over the Sierra Nevada range, requiring a tunnel more than 300 feet long to be built on a curve. In 1886, commercial photographer J. Crockwell toured the railroad and captured this scene of a mixed train stopped at the tunnel before it descended into the Owens Valley below.

Locomotive No. 6—the "Hawthorne"—and train are paused at the state line between Nevada and California. The railroad placed large granite markers along the railroad to mark the state line crossing. This view shows the same train seen in the previous photograph paused below the tunnel on Montgomery Pass.

Benton Station was located at the eastern end of Owens Valley. When the railroad reached Benton Station in March 1883, stagecoaches connected with the railroad destined for Bodie and other destinations around Mono Lake. Railroad ties were supplied by the Bodie Railway & Lumber Company to the C&C and shipped by wagon down to Benton Station for the construction of track in Owens Valley. Located at the base of the Sierra Nevada is Benton Hot Spring, a popular destination that continues to draw visitors to this day.

The C&C business car No. 10 in Benton was built in 1896 to replace the smaller business car No. 2. The new car was built for Henry M. Yerington and his family to travel over the line. After the railroad was sold to the Southern Pacific in 1900, the car was rebuilt without the cupola and given a wider platform. The car was named "Esmeralda" by the SP and remained in service until 1942. After retirement, the body was placed on the ground at Keeler and used as a bunkhouse before it was sold. Today, the body of the car is preserved at the Southern California Railway Museum in Perris, California.

Photographs of the Carson & Colorado prior to 1900 are rare. This badly worn photograph by James Crockwell shows a passenger train stopped at Bishop Creek during the late 1880s. Bishop Creek was renamed Laws in 1900 after Robert. J. Laws, who served as superintendent of the railroad at the time.

Locomotive No. 6, the "Hawthorne," and crew pose for a photograph in Keeler around 1886. Keeler was originally called Hawley after a local farmer. In 1880, the Owens Lake Mining and Milling Company constructed a new mill at Hawley for processing silver ore from the Cerro Gordo Mines in the mountains to the east. Julius M. Keeler, an agent for the mining, company laid out the townsite, and Hawley was renamed Keeler after him.

Darius Ogden Mills established the Inyo Development Company to build a soda ash plant on the eastern shore of Owens Lake in Keeler. Large evaporation ponds (called vats) were constructed along the shore. These vats were filled with the alkali water from Owens Lake and allowed to dry, and the concentrates were harvested for processing. The plant was an important industry along the railroad and continued operation until 1920.

CARSON AND COLORADO RAILWAY.

TIME TABLE No. 40.

TO TAKE EFFECT MONDAY, OCTOBER 23, 1899, AT 6.00 A. M.

For the government and information of employés only.

5 FREIGHT.	3 Bishop and Keeler EXPRESS AND FREIGHT.	1 Bodie and Keeler EXPRESS.	Miles from Mound House.		STATIONS.	Miles from Keeler and Hawthorne.		2 San Francisco & Virginia EXPRESS.	4 San Francisco EXPRESS AND FREIGHT.	6 FREIGHT.
		10.40 AM LV	0	0	Lv. **MOUND HOUSE** Ar 6.0	100	293	5.10 PM AR		
		11.15	6	6	DAYTON 12.0	94	287	4.35		
		12.00 NOON	18	18	CLIFTON 8.0	82	275	3.50		
		12.30 PM	26	26	FT. CHURCHILL 12.0	74	267	3.20		
		1.10 1.30	38	38	WABUSKA 4.0	62	255	2.40 2.20		
		1.45	42	42	* CLEAVER 3.0	58	251	2.05		
		1.55	45	45	MASON 9.0	55	248	**1.55**		
		2.20	54	54	* RIO VISTA 11.0	46	239	1.30		
		3.00	65	65	SCHURZ 13.0	35	228	12.45 PM		
		3.40	78	78	* GILLIS 22.0	22	215	12.00 NOON		
		4.50 PM AR	100	100	Ar. **HAWTHORNE** Lv	0	193	10.50 AM LV		
	6.00 AM LV		100		Lv. **HAWTHORNE** Ar 13.2		193		7.25 PM AR	
	6.37		113		* KINKEAD 11.8		180		6.48	
	7.10		125		LUNING 6.0		168		6.15	
	7.30		131		* NEW BOSTON 6.0		162		5.55	
	7.50		137		SODAVILLE 5.0		156		5.35	
	8.10		142		RHODES 8.0		151		5.15	
	8.50		150		BELLEVILLE 2.0		143		4.35	
	9.00		152		JUNCTION 6.0		141		4.25	
	9.30 9.40				Ar **CANDELARIA STA** Lv				4.00 3.50	
	10.10		152		6.0 JUNCTION 15.0		141		3.25	
	11.10		167		BASALT 8.0		126		2.25	
	12.00 NOON		175		SUMMIT 8.0		118		1.35	
	12.50 PM		183		QUEEN 10.0		110		12.55 PM	
	1.30		193		BENTON STA 11.0		100		11.50	
	2.10		204		HAMMILL 20.0		89		11.00	
	3.10		224		Ar. **BISHOP STA** Lv		69		9.50 AM	
	3.15 PM		224		Lv. **BISHOP STA** Ar 15.0		69		9.45	
	4.05		239		ALVORD 14.0		54		8.55	
	4.50		253		ABERDEEN STA 14.0		40		8.10	
	5.35		267		INDEPENDENCE STA 14.0		26		7.25	
	6.20		281		LONE PINE STA 9.0		12		6.40	
	6.50		290		* SWANSEA 3.0		3		6.10	
	7.00 PM AR		293		Ar. **KEELER** Lv		0		6.00 AM LV	

C. P. MENGEL is the authorized Train Dispatcher.
Full Faced Figures denote meeting and passing places.
All trains must register at Junction.
The attention of employés is particularly called to the Rules and Regulations printed on the back of this card, as important changes have been made.

Trains Nos. 1 and 2 run daily.
Train No. 3 runs Mondays, Wednesdays and Fridays.
Train No. 4 runs Tuesdays, Thursdays and Saturdays.
All trains must slow speed to six (6) miles per hour crossing trestle bridges between Belleville and Candelaria, and passing through Laughton Cañon.

* Flag stations.

H. M. YERINGTON, Genl. Supt. R. J. LAWS, Asst. Supt.

The Carson & Colorado Timetable 40 from 1899 shows the regular trains that ran on the railroad shortly after completion. Despite being 300 miles in length, the railroad only operated two regular passenger trains from Mound House to Hawthorne. The express passenger trains ran daily as far as Hawthorne. Passengers headed south made an overnight stop in Hawthorne where they boarded a mixed train the next morning to continue their journey. Mixed trains operated three times a week each way with overnight stops at Keeler or Hawthorne. Passengers destined for the mining camp of Bodie boarded a stagecoach for the remainder of their trip. (Courtesy of the Stephen E. Drew collection.)

Two

Tonopah Boom

On May 19, 1900, a prospector by the name of Jim Butler made a discovery that changed the course of Nevada's history. Legends say his wayward burro wandered off into the night. The next morning, he found the animal and picked up a rock to throw at it, which he found heavier than expected and discovered it contained silver ore. He filed eight claims that August, and the mines produced nearly $750,000 in gold and silver in the first year. The camp became known as Tonopah from the name given to the area by the Shoshone: *tonampaa*, meaning "thorny bush, hiding spring."

The Carson & Colorado Railway was the nearest freight connection to Tonopah, and the increased traffic from the camp strained the railroad's original equipment. To meet the demand for additional cars, SP started importing equipment from its narrow-gauge lines in California in 1902. The Tonopah boom soon provided SP with a return on its investment.

Heavy freight created a major bottleneck at Mound House, where the contents of standard-gauge cars had to be transferred to narrow-gauge cars. Freight traveled via the C&C to Sodaville and sometimes Candelaria, where it transferred to freight teams for the remainder of the trip to Tonopah. Eastern investors incorporated the Tonopah Railroad to connect with the C&C in 1903, by which trains could travel direct to Tonopah, interchanging equipment between the roads.

Conversion of the 140 miles of track from Mound House to Tonopah Junction to standard gauge began in October 1904. To remove the final bottleneck with Tonopah, SP offered to purchase the Virginia & Truckee Railroad. When the V&T refused to sell, SP chose to build a new route bypassing the connection at Mound House. In 1905, SP formed a subsidiary, the Nevada & California Railroad (N&C), to build the new standard-gauge connection. The new line started at Hazen, located 40 miles east of Reno on the transcontinental main line. It was constructed south of Churchill, where it joined the original C&C main line. The Carson & Colorado Railway was then sold on May 11, 1906, to the N&C and dissolved as a corporation.

In 1905, commercial photographer J.E. Stimson of Wyoming captured this southern view of Mound House, looking north along the V&T main line. The building in the foreground is the Western Ore Sampling Works. The former narrow-gauge C&C freight yard, visible on the right-hand side of the image, was converted to standard gauge in 1904.

Sodaville is near a natural spring and was a water stop on the railroad. The large freight house on the right was the nearest freight connection to Tonopah. Within a few short years, Sodaville went from a lonely whistle stop on the railroad to the busiest terminal on the C&C. This photograph shows the southern end of Sodaville around 1902 after the new warehouse was constructed for Tonopah boom traffic. (Courtesy of the Stephen E. Drew collection.)

Hawthorne was a busy place in the first five years of the boom period. C&C established a substantial facility for servicing locomotives and cars when it arrived in 1881. In the distance on the left are the dual enginehouses and other shop buildings constructed after the C&C arrived. (Courtesy of the Brian Norden Collection.)

SP 1024 and crew pose alongside the freight depot in Hawthorne, Nevada, around 1904. The H.K. Porter Company of Pittsburg, Pennsylvania, built the locomotive for the San Joaquin & Sierra Nevada Railroad of California in 1882. SP acquired that line in 1883 and converted it to standard gauge in 1899. No. 1024 operated briefly in Nevada before it was scrapped in 1907.

To meet the demands of the Tonopah boom traffic, the Southern Pacific brought in a variety of locomotives from its other narrow-gauge lines. South Pacific Coast Railroad (SPC) 22 and crew pose in the yard at Hawthorne around 1904. The Baldwin Locomotive Works built the handsome 4-6-0 in 1889. It was transferred to the Nevada & California Railroad in July 1906, becoming N&C No. 15. (Courtesy of the Stephen E. Drew collection.)

Nevada & California Railroad combine No. 7 takes up the rear of a passenger train. The V&T shops in Carson City built the car in 1883 as C&C No. 7. Shortly after this photograph was taken, No. 7 was repurposed into maintenance-of-way service as derrick tender/boarding car No. 7. It was retired from service on November 28, 1915. (Courtesy of the Stephen E. Drew collection.)

Tonopah Junction was a lonely point between two busy railroads. Despite the importance of the junction, the facilities located there were sparse. The C&C maintained only a couple of passing sidings here while the Tonopah & Goldfield had a telegraph office, water tank, and section gang housing. Here, a C&C passenger train passes through Tonopah Junction on its way to the Owens Valley.

E.W. Smith took this photograph of the loading track on the north side of the Tonopah depot. This busy 1904 view shows a variety of cars from the former Carson & Colorado along with boxcars brought from the South Pacific Coast Railway.

Tonopah became the largest mining boom since the Comstock Lode. To supply the needs of the growing camp, the Tonopah Railroad was constructed by eastern capitalists to connect with the Carson & Colorado. This panoramic photograph shows the lower portion of the yard in Tonopah and the menagerie of railroad cars in use on the two railroads. Cars from the South Pacific Coast,

Northern Railway, Carson & Colorado, and the Tonopah Railroad can be seen. On the right edge of the photograph, a passenger train led by a C&C 4-4-0 is making its way through the yard to the depot. (Courtesy of the University of Las Vegas Special Collections.)

The depot at Tonopah was built using Southern Pacific plans. It was newly built at the time this photograph was taken in 1905. The railroad yard is filled with a variety of freight cars wearing different reporting marks. (Photograph by Joseph E. Stimson; courtesy of the Wyoming State Archives.)

To the north of the depot was a series of platforms for unloading freight cars. Goods delivered to the bustling mining camp are seen in the center of this view awaiting transport by wagon. (Photograph by Joseph E. Stimson; courtesy of the Wyoming State Archives.)

Sacks of ore await shipment on loading platforms in Tonopah. Leased locomotive Denver & Rio Grande Railroad No. 66 pulls a flatcar from the San Joaquin & Sierra Nevada Railroad. Three cabooses of the Tonopah Railroad are standing along the transfer platforms. These cabooses operated on the narrow gauge but were converted to standard gauge after 1905 and used on the Tonopah & Goldfield. (Photograph by Joseph E. Stimson; courtesy of the Wyoming State Archives.)

Flatcars lettered for three different railroads are visible in the postcard of the Montana Tonopah Mine's Ore tipple: a C&C LaMothe patent "pipe" flatcar, Tonopah Railroad flatcar No. 1014, and a South Pacific Coast flatcar No. 873, a 30-foot-long car built in Sacramento for the SPC.

The Tonopah boom brought substantial business to the railroad. This photograph, taken on Montgomery Pass in 1904, shows the construction camp for a new road over the pass. In the background, a C&C train descends on the pass with two former South Pacific Coast Railroad 10-wheeler locomotives with locomotive No. 18 leading the train. Among the cars in the train are two Tonopah Railroad boxcars mixed with C&C cars destined for the Owens Valley.

Queen was located where the route over Montgomery Pass entered the Owens Valley. Here, a water stop and siding were constructed for trains headed over the pass. Teamster Jim Morley is delivering a load of cordwood. After the SP gained control of the C&C, the locomotives were converted to burning coal. Just beyond the wood pile, two locomotives, including former South Pacific Coast Railroad No. 12, are paused, and the coal loaded in its tender can be seen.

Open cattle ranges along the railroad created daily hazards for railroad crews. C&C No. 8 helps clear up a wreck caused by a train hitting a bull on the track. Early stock cars like those seen in this view had open tops, resembling little more than modified flatcars. Visible at the end of the train is combine No. 25, which transferred to the N&C in 1906.

Former C&C caboose coach No. 2 is seen on the Tonopah Railroad, which has recently been changed to standard gauge. The car was built as a caboose coach in 1881 and rebuilt with a partial clerestory roof for use as a business car in 1882 for Henry M. Yerington and later by R.J. Laws. In 1900, it was transferred to the Inyo Development Company and sold to the Tonopah Railroad in 1904. On the Tonopah Railroad, it was given the number 5 and used as a business car before it was retired as a bunkhouse in Millers, Nevada. (Courtesy of the Dave Garcia collection.)

The Montana-Tonopah mine was one of several mining operations served by the Tonopah Railroad. This postcard view shows a string of narrow-gauge cars below the mill in the lower-right corner. Visible are a former South Pacific Coast Railroad combination boxcar and two tank cars built from C&C LaMothe patent "pipe" flatcars. (Courtesy of the Dennis Burke collection.)

The Tonopah Railroad purchased three locomotives from the Baldwin Locomotive Works in 1904. No. 4, seen here, was the only brand-new locomotive built for the railroad. After the Tonopah Railroad was converted to standard gauge, it was sold to the Sumpter Valley Railway in Oregon, where it remained in service until 1929. It was stored for several years and finally scraped during the 1940s.

Three

Nevada & California Railroad

Conversion of the northern portion of the N&C reached Tonopah Junction in July 1905. On the news of the conversion, the Tonopah Railroad converted to standard gauge in August. The new standard-gauge connection from Hazen, known as the Hazen Cutoff, opened for traffic on September 1, 1905. The former C&C line from Mound House to Churchill, now standard gauge, became the SP's Mound House Branch. During conversion, Hawthorne was bypassed to shorten the trip to Tonopah. A new station called Thorne was constructed several miles north on the new line from Hawthorne, replacing the former C&C station.

The shop facilities at Hawthorne were closed, and a new facility was planned closer to Tonopah Junction. SP's initial plan was to construct the new terminal at Sodaville, but land speculators drove up the price of land. Instead, SP established a new terminal 10 miles to the north. The new town of Mina was named for Ferminia Sarras, a famed prospector known regionally as the "Copper Queen." New facilities were constructed, including an enginehouse for narrow- and standard-gauge locomotives, a large interchange yard, stockyard, and freight and passenger depots, along with a sprawling company town for employees.

Gold discoveries in Goldfield, Nevada, led the investors of the Tonopah Railroad to construct the standard-gauge Goldfield Railroad in early 1905. The two railroads merged into the Tonopah & Goldfield Railroad (T&G) on November 1, 1905. The T&G had trackage rights over the SP line between Tonopah Junction and Mina, where its locomotives were turned and serviced at the SP's facilities.

In 1908, a standard-gauge branch was constructed north from Mojave as part of the N&C, which finally established a southern connection with the SP system. The new line, known as the Jawbone Branch, met the narrow gauge at a place named Owenyo (a portmanteau of Owens and Inyo) in 1910. Construction of the new line coincided with that of the Los Angeles Aqueduct in the Owens Valley. The N&C was sold to the Central Pacific Railway and leased back to the Southern Pacific Railroad in February 1912. It became the Mina Branch of the SP's Salt Lake Division.

Depot at Hazen was constructed in 1905 on the Central Pacific's transcontinental route east of Reno, Nevada. Hazen served as the starting point for two branches of the SP system—the Nevada & California Railroad from Hazen to Mojave and the Fallon Branch from Hazen to Fallon. (Courtesy of the Stephen E. Drew collection.)

Located where the Carson & Colorado's main line turned south from the Carson River canyon was a small station called Churchill. When the Hazen Branch was constructed, Churchill became the junction point with the C&C main line. This photograph shows the trim little depot and outbuildings after the completion of the Hazen connection and the conversion of the former C&C to standard gauge. (Courtesy of the Stephen E. Drew collection.)

The depot at Mina was built in 1905 following Southern Pacific designs. It was a Common Standard Plan No. 22. The depot remained in place after passenger service was discontinued over the Mina Branch. After railroad service, it became a café and office building for many years. The depot was accidentally destroyed by fire in the late 1960s.

The regular westbound passenger train arrives at Benton pulled by the first locomotive to carry the No. 9. Built for the South Pacific Coast Railroad in 1887 as No. 21, it was transferred to the C&C in 1904. It became N&C No. 9 in 1905 but served only a few short years on the Mina Branch before it was retired and scrapped in 1910.

A passenger train stops at Benton before ascending Montgomery Pass. Passenger trains over the pass were not required to take on helper locomotives. Parked near the depot is square water car No. 59, one of three similar cars that came to the railroad from California. They are built in a similar design to cars used on Southern Pacific's standard-gauge lines. (Courtesy of the Dennis Burke collection.)

Communities along the railroad were accustomed to the railroad as part of their daily life. These two photographs show members of an unidentified family at Benton waiting for the train in the early 20th century (above). Members of the same family stand on the rear platform of a passenger train as they leave for destinations unknown (below).

Locomotive No. 7 prepares to leave Mina with a eastbound train. Built in 1881 for the Carson & Colorado and named "Benton," it was transferred to the N&C in 1905. It became Southern Pacific No. 7 in 1912 and remained in operation until 1929. It was scrapped in Sacramento in January 1932.

Nevada & California No. 1, the former C&C "Candelaria" with a short mixed train, is seen near Montgomery Pass. The locomotive remained on the N&C until 1906 when it was sold to the Eureka & Palisade Railroad in northern Nevada. There, it operated until 1912 when it was traded to the Sumpter Valley Railway and subsequently transferred to the Oregon Lumber Company in eastern Oregon. It became the lumber company's No. 102 and was used to haul supply trains until it was scrapped in 1940.

The settlement of Laws is located five miles from Bishop on the eastern side of the Owens River. Several wagons and an early automobile are gathered around the depot in this c. 1912 view. A string of former South Pacific Coast Railroad boxcars can be seen on the siding just north of the depot. (Courtesy of the Dennis Burke collection.)

Owenyo was a remote location when the Jawbone Branch was constructed. The first depot located there was a former standard-gauge boxcar body placed on the ground in 1910. As Owenyo grew in importance as a transfer point, new facilities were constructed to meet demands, and the depot was replaced with a new structure in the 1920s.

During the first decades of the 20th century, the Nevada Power, Mining, and Milling Company began construction on a series of powerhouses and reservoirs to supply them. Here, at Laws, materials for the Bishop Creek Hydroelectric Project are being unloaded for shipment to the powerhouse construction site. The Nevada Power, Mining, and Milling Company eventually became part of Southern California Edison. (Courtesy of the Southern California Edison Collection.)

Generator components for the Rush Creek Hydroelectric Project are being transferred at Benton. The Nevada Power, Mining, and Milling Company constructed a warehouse and transfer crane in Benton for the project. Materials were shipped to Benton by rail and transferred to a truck for the 40-mile drive by dirt road to June Lake, where they were used to construct the powerhouse. (Courtesy of the Southern California Edison Collection.)

Four

The Slim Princess

The future looked bright for the Mina Branch after merging into the Southern Pacific. In June 1913, overnight Pullman service was established between Mojave and Owenyo over the recently completed Jawbone Branch. It was SP's general passenger agent, F.A. Batturs, who coined the moniker "Slim Princess" for the narrow-gauge line after the new service was established. Mining activity in the Tonopah and Goldfield districts reached its peak that same year. SP shelved plans to convert the narrow gauge between Owenyo and Mina to standard gauge.

Since 1908, the construction of the Los Angeles Aqueduct had been progressing northward into Owens Valley. In 1913, the completion of the Los Angeles Aqueduct diverted much of the water from Owens Valley. As the valley ecosystem began to dry up, so did the agricultural industry, leading to a decline in freight revenue for the railroad. This was compounded by the encroachment of the automobile and trucks, along with the construction of paved highways, which linked the communities on the west side of the valley.

Passenger service continued to run daily, except Sundays, from Owenyo to Laws. With revenue declining, the mail contract over Montgomery Pass was lost in 1929. Passenger service over the line was reduced to a lowly combine passenger car on the end of the semiweekly freight train. In 1934, the largely idle Candelaria Branch was abandoned along with the former narrow-gauge Mound House Branch.

In 1935, the railroad hauled a mere 59 passengers over Montgomery Pass. The final train over the pass brought the remaining equipment from Mina to Owens Valley on February 16, 1938, and the 50-mile stretch from Tonopah Junction to Benton was abandoned. The line between Benton and Laws was soon abandoned in 1943. With the removal of the link to the Mina Branch, the line became known as the Keeler Branch and operated as part of the SP's San Joaquin Division. What was once a 300-mile-long continuous system was reduced to an isolated 70-mile stretch between Laws and Keeler.

Locomotive No. 18 switches freight cars at the Mina freight depot. No. 18 was built for the Nevada–California–Oregon Railway (N-C-O) by the Baldwin Locomotive Works in 1911. On the N-C-O it carried the number 12 and came to the Mina Branch in 1928. SP changed the number to 18 because there was already a locomotive numbered 12 on the roster. It remained in service until July 1955 when it was donated to Inyo County for display in Independence, California.

The transfer platform at Mina was located on the western edge of the yard by the freight depot. Standard-gauge cars were spotted on the siding at right while the narrow-gauge cars were lined up on the opposite side. The transfer platform was built directly to the south of the freight depot. (Photograph by Gerald Best.)

The view looking north from the roof of the Mina enginehouse provides a glimpse of the narrow- and standard-gauge equipment in the yard. In the distance on the main line an eastbound train prepares to leave for Montgomery Pass. The two-story building in the foreground is the railroad storekeeper's warehouse; adjacent to it in the distance was a small park area maintained by the railroad.

The eastbound triweekly mixed train leaves Mina for Montgomery Pass. The train is passing alongside the heavy cranes for unloading cars on the south end of town. Like the preceding image, this view was taken from the roof of the Mina enginehouse, this time looking south.

Locomotive No. 14 leads a train headed east as it navigates through the yard at Mina in 1936. This photograph was taken along the north wall of the enginehouse. The ramp for the transfer platform can be seen on the left. Silhouetted on the right-hand side of this photograph is a storage rack for spare freight car parts.

Mina was the center of operation for much of the Slim Princess's life and a variety of equipment could be found there. Coach No. 5, flanger No. 108, and caboose No. 1 are seen in Mina during the late 1930s. Coach No. 5 was sold to Disney animator Ward Kimball in 1938 for his Grizzly Flats Railroad. Today, the coach is preserved at the Southern California Railway Museum.

The largest locomotive to operate on the Southern Pacific Narrow Gauge (SPNG) was second No. 1, seen here departing Mina on a cold day. It was built for the Nevada–California–Oregon Railway as No. 14 in 1911. It came to the SPNG in 1927 and was used primarily as a helper locomotive, providing additional pulling capacity to trains over Montgomery Pass. It was prone to derailing, particularly in the winter, and was sold to the Nevada County Narrow Gauge Railroad in 1934. In 1942, it was sold to the US Navy for use at Pearl Harbor. After World War II, the locomotive was scrapped.

Locomotive No. 9 waits on the main line preparing to depart Mina for the Owens Valley. No. 9 came to the railroad from the Nevada–California–Oregon Railway after the Southern Pacific purchased that railroad and converted it to standard gauge in 1928. It was the last steam locomotive to operate on the Southern Pacific Narrow Gauge and was donated to Inyo County in April 1960.

Livestock was an important commodity on the railroad during the fall and spring. Locomotive Nos. 16, 12, and 18 lead a stock train out of Mina destined for the Owens Valley.

Another triple-header led by locomotive Nos. 18, 14, and 8 leads a 20-car train upgrade out of the Soda Springs Valley in December 1936. Soon, the train will reach Belleville before continuing over Montgomery Pass.

Locomotive No. 5 prepares to leave Mina at the head of the triweekly passenger train. Former C&C No. 5 was one of several locomotives rebuilt by the Southern Pacific in the early 1920s. Modifications included a new boiler, which increased their operating pressure. (Courtesy of the Stephen E. Drew collection.)

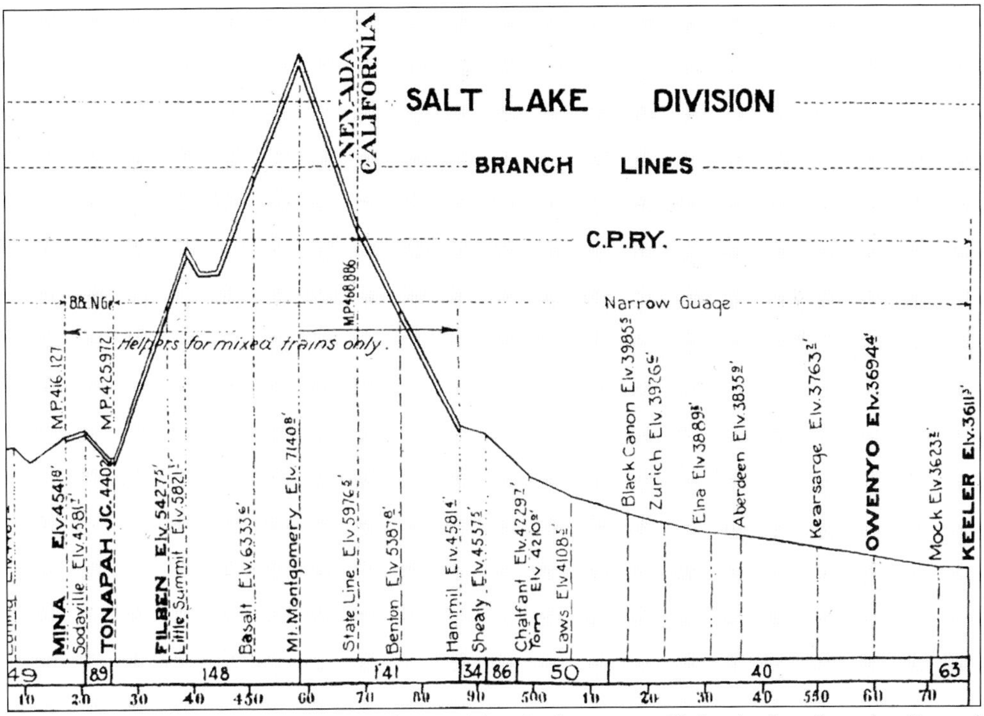

The route of Montgomery Pass crossed a 7,105-foot-high summit, 73 feet higher than the Central Pacific Railroad's transcontinental line over Donner Pass. As the grade wound up and down the pass, it maintained a maximum 2.25 percent grade.

A triple-headed train stops at Basalt to take on water before ascending the eastern slope of Montgomery Pass. The remote station of Basalt had no formal depot but served as the division point for section crews on the railroad who lived in the small assortment of structures located there. Water for the tank and the settlement was piped in from the reservoir system built to supply the town of Candelaria. (Courtesy of the California State Railroad Museum, T.L. Williamson Collection.)

Located at an elevation of 6,100 feet, Basalt was the last water stop on the eastern side of Montgomery Pass. Located at a high elevation, the winter in the open desert was forbiddingly cold. Wooden water tanks like this one were prone to leak and, in cold weather, grew impressive icicles like the ones seen here. (Photograph by Al Phelps.)

A double-headed freight train led by No. 5 has paused at the Mount Montgomery station. In 1918, the body of a baggage car was placed at the site to serve as a freight house. Prior to this the location only had a telegraph agent's office. (Courtesy of the Dave Garcia collection.)

On July 3, 1923, two 4-4-0 locomotives assigned as helpers to the regular triweekly train derailed while descending Montgomery Pass. Locomotive Nos. 5 and 7 were cut off the train at Mount Montgomery station and run light ahead of the freight train. The derailment severely injured the fireman of the lead locomotive, requiring amputation of his lower legs. He died the next day at a hospital in Los Angeles.

An eastbound freight train passes through the Montgomery Pass tunnel, shrouded by the escaping steam on a cold day (above). Moments later, the train rounds the horseshoe curve just below the Montgomery Pass tunnel as it continues the descent into the Owens Valley. (Both, courtesy of the Arthur Haig Collection.)

A freight train led by 10-wheeler Nos. 17 and 9 prepares to leave Mina in the 1930s. In the train behind No. 9 is auxiliary water car No. 61. Water cars like these were essential in the desert for carrying additional water for the locomotives.

Locomotive Nos. 9 and 22 take on water at Hammil with a westbound train headed for Mina. Hammil was the southern end of the helper district headed over Montgomery Pass. A water tank and wye track for turning locomotives were established here.

The weekly mixed train pauses in front of the Mount Montgomery station before descending down to the Owens Valley. On this occasion, two railfans caught the train at the pass and photographed one of the last mixed trains over this section of the line before it was abandoned in 1938. In the final years, service was limited to a single weekly mixed train from Mina to Owenyo.

Combine No. 8 is on the end of the train stopped in Montgomery Pass. There were no services on the summit, but this railfan is enjoying his canned lunch on the end platform after boarding the train for the trip down into the Owens Valley.

The steep grades over Montgomery Pass necessitated stops to cool the brakes of the locomotives and freight cars. The same train seen on the preceding page is making the required stop to inspect the brakes before continuing down to Owens Valley. Visible near the tail of the train is the old wagon road over Montgomery Pass.

The route down Montgomery Pass wound along the hillside into Owens Valley. This view shows the highway crossing in the foreground, which wound up the higher path above the railroad. In the distance, the railroad grade can be seen as it wraps around this loop above and below the Montgomery Pass tunnel.

Hammil was one of several locations with livestock pens served by the railroad. Stock chutes like these were found at Benton, Hammil, Chalfant, Laws, Monola, Kearsarge, and Aberdeen. Livestock could be taken to Mina or Owenyo, where it was transferred to standard-gauge cars.

Hammil was at the southern end of the helper district over Montgomery Pass. Despite its importance to the railroad, there was no depot building. The railroad maintained a water tank, wye for turning locomotives, and section houses for track workers here.

Shealy was the location of a siding and loading ramp that served the Champion Mine. The operation was founded by Dr. Joseph Jeffery, who partnered with the Champion Spark Plug Company to mine andalusite used in the production of ceramics. The mine was located in the White Mountains east of the railroad and operated between 1918 and 1945. Sacked ore was carried by mule down to the base camp located four miles east of the railroad. The ore was transferred to a truck for the final leg of the trip and loaded into narrow-gauge cars.

The Pine Creek Tungsten Mine, located high in the mountains above Bishop, was operated by the US Vanadium Corporation and, later, the Union Carbide Corporation. Tungsten ore was shipped from the mine by truck to Laws, where it was transferred to the narrow gauge. The mine outlived the railroad and continued operation until 2001. (Courtesy of the California State Library.)

This boxcar hotel was built in Owenyo in 1922. The structure was comprised of several retired boxcar bodies with a large common area in the center. The hotel was primarily used by railroad employees. In later years it was referred to as the Owenyo Hotel until it closed in 1950. (Courtesy of the Taylor Rush collection.)

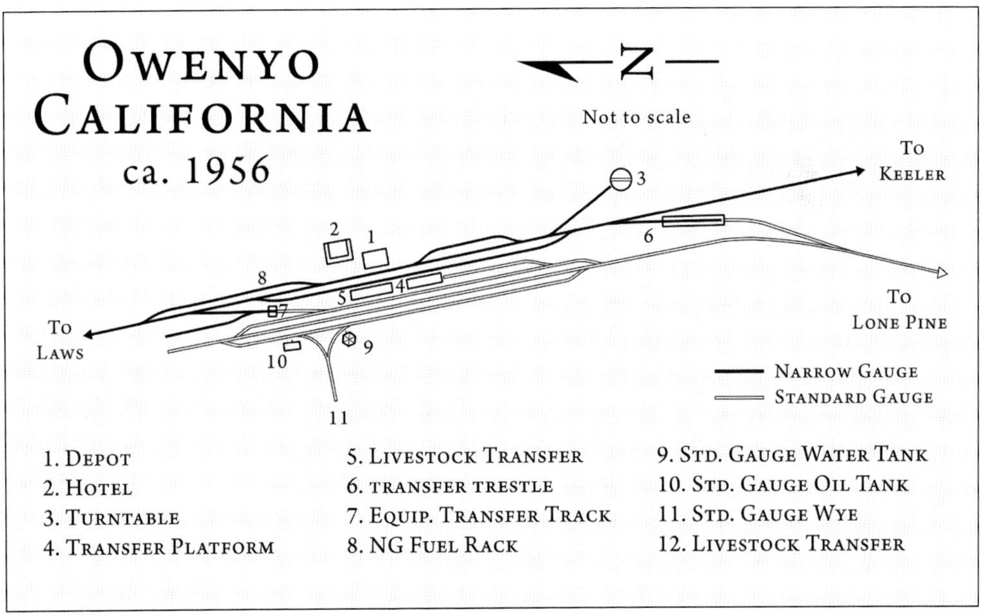

Owenyo was the interchange point between the standard gauge and narrow gauge. This track map shows the overall layout of the railroad facilities in Owenyo during the final days of the railroad.

Keeler was the southern terminal of the railroad until it was scrapped in 1960. The view above shows the west side of town, looking toward the railroad facilities during the 1920s. Keeler was home to a single-stall enginehouse seen in the distance (below). The wooden enginehouse was built in the 1880s and located at the end of the spur off the main line. When the railroad arrived in Keeler, it built a wye south of town for turning locomotives thus avoiding the need for a turntable. (Above, courtesy of the Dennis Burke collection; below, courtesy of the California State Library.)

Construction of Tinemaha Reservoir began in 1927. An earthen dam was built across the valley to retain water from the Owens River for the Los Angeles Aqueduct system. The construction project utilized its own narrow-gauge railroad to move fill dirt to the site. In this view looking north, a construction train is seen unloading fill. The Owens River can be seen in the distance, where a row of trees is visible. (Courtesy of the California State Archives.)

Located two miles beyond Keeler was Natural Soda Products (NSP). The company marked the southernmost point on the railroad. Though SP handled the switching of cars, the final stretch of track was owned by NSP. Soda ash was shipped in boxcars from here to Owenyo, where it was transferred to standard-gauge cars. The company ceased operation in 1952. (Courtesy of the Dennis Burke collection.)

Located in the mountains to the east of Keeler is the famed mining camp of Cerro Gordo ("fat hill" in Spanish). In December 1868, regular shipments of silver bullion to Los Angeles began. Silver ingots 18 inches long and weighing 85 pounds were worth $20–$35. By the 1880s, the town was booming, and the Carson & Colorado became the closest railroad connection when the line was completed to Keeler. Silver mining declined at Cerro Gordo at the end of the 19th century and mines lay dormant.

In 1914, the Cerro Gordo Mines Company began mining lead and zinc in addition to low-grade silver ore. The company constructed a Leschen wire rope aerial tramway to move ore down the mountains to a transfer terminal in Keeler. Narrow-gauge cars loaded with ore were sent to Owenyo for transfer to the standard gauge. Ore was then shipped to United States Smelting and Refining Company in Tooele, Utah, for processing. At its peak, the tramway shipped 20 tons of zinc ore per day down to the railroad.

Tram buckets of the Cerro Gordo aerial tramway stand silently in this view looking north from the remains of the smelter above Keeler during the 1950s. Shipment of zinc ore continued into the early 1920s until the Cerro Gordo Mines Company ceased operation. National Soda Products acquired the property and began shipping 80 tons of limestone per day over the tramway. Shipments over the tramway continued until 1933. The tramway system remained intact after ore shipments ceased. The tramway terminal in Keeler was removed in 1959. Much of the tramway was dismantled and moved to Candelaria, but a section complete with tramcar remains in the canyon at the time of this writing.

The Mount Whitney station was the location of the original Lone Pine depot. In 1901, the station was renamed Mount Whitney. A new depot for Lone Pine was built on the Jawbone Branch in 1909. The depot at Mount Whitney station was closed in 1911, and the station agent moved to the new Lone Pine depot.

This view of Zurich from the south, taken prior to 1947, shows a harp switch stand still in use with a stub derail. Derails are used to prevent cars from rolling down the track in the event the brakes have failed or were released on accident or due to mischief. The open rail causes the car to simply derail onto the ground and prevent catastrophic damage to other equipment.

The station of Kearsarge was originally named Independence after the settlement of the same name on the western side of the Owens River when the C&C arrived in 1883. Independence was renamed Citrus in April 1900 and later renamed Kearsarge in April 1911. (Photograph by John Cummings; courtesy of the Herman Darr collection.)

Locomotive No. 18 leads an eastbound train toward Owenyo past the Kearsarge depot. The station agency closed in 1932, and the depot was removed in December 1955. (Courtesy of the Stephen E. Drew collection.)

Locomotive No. 9 switches a string of boxcars at Natural Soda Products south of Keeler during the 1940s. Soda ash was loaded directly into boxcars at the facility through a pair of small doors on the sides of each car located along the roof. At Owenyo, the cars were unloaded manually into the bulk material loader and transferred to standard-gauge cars. (Courtesy of the Dennis Burke collection.)

Locomotive No. 8 with a light train heads westbound toward Owenyo from Keeler. Between Keeler and Swansea, the railroad crossed through sand dunes, requiring special operations.

The depot at Laws went through several changes over the years. When built, it was a 20-by-60-foot structure. In 1918, the building was extended 16 feet in length. In preparation for the planned conversion to standard gauge, the roof eave alongside the track was cut back to provide clearance for standard-gauge equipment.

Locomotive No. 8 leads a train through the Laws yard in 1940. Compared with other yards along the railroad, Laws's location near the Owens River allowed grass to grow, providing a stark contrast to other stations on the line.

The Mina enginehouse was a standard design used across the SP system during the early 20th century. Similar structures were built at Hazen, Montello, and Imlay. In this pair of photographs are locomotive No. 8 (above) and No. 14 (below) inside the structure. (Courtesy of the Martin E. Hansen collection.)

MINA SUB-DIVISION

(Narrow Gauge)

EASTWARD — **WESTWARD**

Capacity of sidings in car lengths	THIRD CLASS 614 Freight	SECOND CLASS 612 Mixed	SECOND CLASS 124 T. & G. Tonopah Express Mixed	Distance from San Francisco	Time Table No. 48 April 1, 1935 Mina Branch STATIONS	Distance from Keeler	SECOND CLASS 123 T. & G. San Francisco Passenger Mixed	SECOND CLASS 611 Mixed	THIRD CLASS 613 Freight
	Leave Daily Ex. Sunday	Leave Tuesday	Leave Daily Ex. Monday				Arrive Daily Ex. Sunday	Arrive Wednesday	Arrive Daily Ex. Sunday
Yard POWYBK		7.00 AM	4.40 AM	417.0	TO-R MINA 3.5	160.2	s 11.10 AM	s 7.40 PM	
Spur 4		f 7.10	f 4.50	420.5	SODAVILLE 4.5	156.7	f 11.00	f 7.30	
Spur 4		f	f	425.0	RHODES 1.0	152.2	f	f	
Yard		s 7.30	s 5.05 AM	426.0	R TONOPAH JCT. 6.4	151.2	10.40 AM	s 7.15	
20 PW		f 7.59		432.4	BELLEVILLE 3.0	144.8		f 6.45	
Y		f 8.11		435.4	FILBEN 3.3	141.8		f	
Spur 2		f		438.7	LITTLE SUMMIT 6.1	138.5		f	
Spur 10		f		444.8	RAYDEL 5.6	132.4		f	
18 PW		s 9.20		450.4	BASALT 7.7	126.8		s 5.25	
24 PY		s 10.00		458.1	MT. MONTGOMERY 8.6	119.1		s 4.35	
15 PW		s 10.50		466.7	QUEEN 2.2	110.5		s 3.55	
				468.9	STATE LINE 7.1	108.3			
24 P		s 11.30 AM		476.0	BENTON 11.0	101.2		s 3.15	
13 YPW		s 12.05 PM		487.0	HAMMIL 2.4	90.2		s 2.35	
12		f		489.4	DEHY 1.9	87.8		f	
4		f 12.15		491.3	SHEALY 7.8	85.9		f 2.15	
14 P		f 12.32		499.1	CHALFANT 2.6	78.1		f 1.55	
12		f		501.7	TOM 5.1	75.5		f	
Yard PO1WK		1.05 1.50		506.8	TO-R LAWS 2.8	70.4		1.30 12.45	
		f		509.6	POLITA 2.1	67.6		f	
8		f 2.02		511.7	BIGELOW 4.4	65.5		f 12.30	
8		f 2.13		516.1	BLACK CANYON 6.6	61.1		f 12.20	
14 P		s 2.35		522.7	ZURICH 2.8	54.5		s 12.05 PM	
9		f 2.42		525.5	MONOLA 1.3	51.7		f 11.51 AM	
10 Y		f 2.45		526.8	BENEME 4.1	50.4		f 11.47	
8		f 2.55		530.9	ELNA 6.0	46.3		f 11.36	
20 PW		f 3.10		536.9 536.2	ABERDEEN 13.9	40.8		f 11.20	
14 PW		s 4.00		550.1	KEARSARGE 5.1	26.4		s 10.45	
8		f 4.10		555.2	MANZANAR 4.6	21.3		f 10.20	
Yard TPK	11.45 AM	s 4.40		559.8	TO-R OWENYO 3.9	16.7		10.10 9.10	9.55 AM
14 P	12.05 PM	f 4.51		563.7	MT. WHITNEY 5.0	12.8		f 9.01	9.45
Spur 67		f		568.7	ALICO 1.5	7.8		f	
Spur 8		f		570.2	DOLOMITE 1.2	6.3		f	
Spur 39		f		571.4	MOCK 0.8	5.1		f	
6	12.35	f 5.11		572.2	TRAMWAY 4.3	4.3		f 8.43	9.05
Yard WYBK	12.50 PM	s 5.25 PM		576.5	TO-R KEELER	0.0		8.30 AM	8.55 AM
	Arrive Daily Ex. Sunday.	Arrive Tuesday	Arrive Daily Ex. Monday		(160.2)		Leave Daily Ex. Sunday	Leave Wednesday	Leave Daily Ex. Sunday
	(1.05)	(10.25)	(0.25)		Time over District		(0.30)	(11.10)	(1.00)
	15.41	15.37	21.00		Average speed per hour		18.00	14.34	16.70

Joint Track Three Rails (Mina – Tonopah Jct.)

Timetable 48, published April 1, 1935, shows the limited service available over the branch at that time. Train Nos. 611 and 612 are the biweekly mixed trains from Mina to Keeler, while train Nos. 613 and 614 operated daily between Owenyo and Keeler.

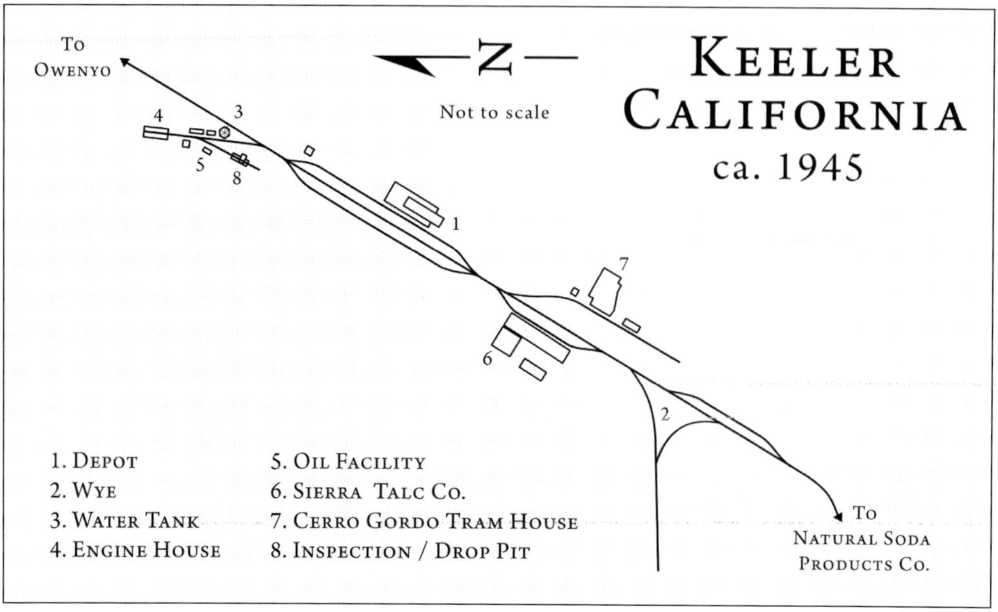

Industries located in Keeler included the Inyo Development Company, situated along the south side of the railroad. The Sierra Talc Company, Natural Soda Products, and several small mining companies owned loading ramps for dumping material into gondolas destined for Owenyo.

The depot at Keeler went through many changes during the railroad's lifetime. In 1917, the original board-and-batten depot was expanded upon, and a two-story depot with quarters for the station agent was added on the south end.

Keeler had a compact outdoor locomotive service facility. In this view, No. 18 is over the drop pit with all of the driving axles removed. No. 9 is under steam ahead of No. 18, while No. 8 can be seen over the inspection pit located at the former wooden enginehouse site. The water tank and pump house were located along the main line and are visible on the right side of this view.

Three locomotives, including Nos. 8 and 17, are seen on the service track in Keeler. A single-stall enginehouse at Keeler was built in 1883 after the railroad arrived. It burned down in 1946. Owing to the desert climate, the railroad chose to not rebuild the structure, and maintenance and minor repairs were performed outdoors in this cramped space.

Hollywood found the Owens Valley to be the perfect filming location for Westerns. The railroad appeared in a variety of motion pictures and Western serials. In 1948, director John Ford selected the Owens Valley as the backdrop for *Three Godfathers*, starring John Wayne, Pedro Armendariz, and Harry Carey Jr. The Slim Princess played an important role in the film. Locomotive No. 9, along with several freight cars and caboose No. 400, starred in the picture. (Both photographs from Argosy Pictures, courtesy of Larry Jensen.)

A legend of Western serial films, Gene Autry filmed in the Owens Valley frequently and produced several features using the railroad. In *The Blazing Sun*, Autry, his horse Champion, and friend Mike pursue a pair of bank robbers. The climax of the film concludes with a shoot-out on the railroad. The film made extensive use of the railroad, including a runaway locomotive sequence where the depot at Keeler was used for the fictional town of Whitewater.

Ties removed from the line over Montgomery Pass are loaded in gondolas at Benton during 1943. Rails and other track material were brought down to Benton prior to shipment to Owenyo for the war effort. (Photograph by Richard Datin.)

In the late 1920s, very little freight traffic was generated in Benton, and the depot agency closed in 1925. The depot was abandoned in February 1943 and removed with the rest of the line north to Mina during that year.

Mount Montgomery was an infrequent destination for passengers and freight. The telegraph office located there closed in 1929 but remained in place after the line over Montgomery Pass was scrapped. In this view, the train order boards have been removed from the signal, indicating the office has been closed. (Courtesy of the Stephen E. Drew collection.)

SP caboose No. 16 and other equipment are being stored in "the pit" track at Owenyo. The pit was dug into the ground to ease the process of transferring oil and gasoline from the standard-gauge track seen in the background at a higher elevation. When the shipment of oil and gasoline ended in the late 1920s, the track was used to store excess equipment in the Owenyo yard.

SP Mikado class No. 3206, assigned to train No. 606, is seen switching at Mina. At the time this photograph was taken, the Mina depot was being used as a café (above). Below, Pilot Peak looms over the Mina enginehouse and the south end of the yard after the narrow gauge was removed in 1942. Although the narrow gauge had been removed, Mina remained an active shipping point on the railroad. (Both, courtesy of the Stephen E. Drew collection.)

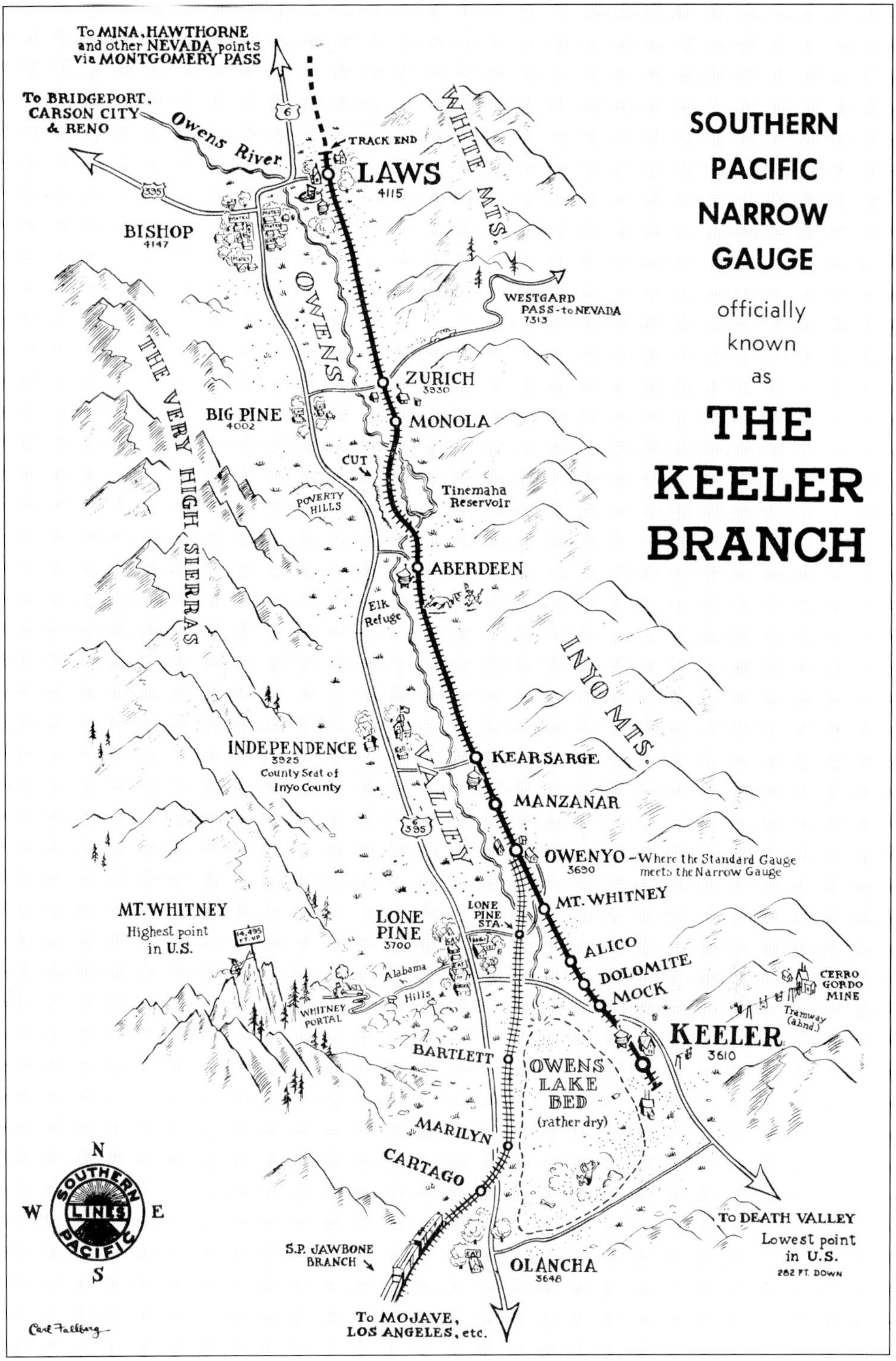

Pictured here is the Keeler Branch in the 1940s, drawn by legendary cartoonist Carl Fallberg. This map provides an overview of the remaining railroad after the track north of Laws was removed in 1943.

Locomotive No. 9 takes a spin on the "armstrong" turntable at Laws. All of the turntables used on the railroad were turned with human power, and the routine seen in these photographs was a daily occurrence. Laws was home to the final turntable on the railroad in the 1950s.

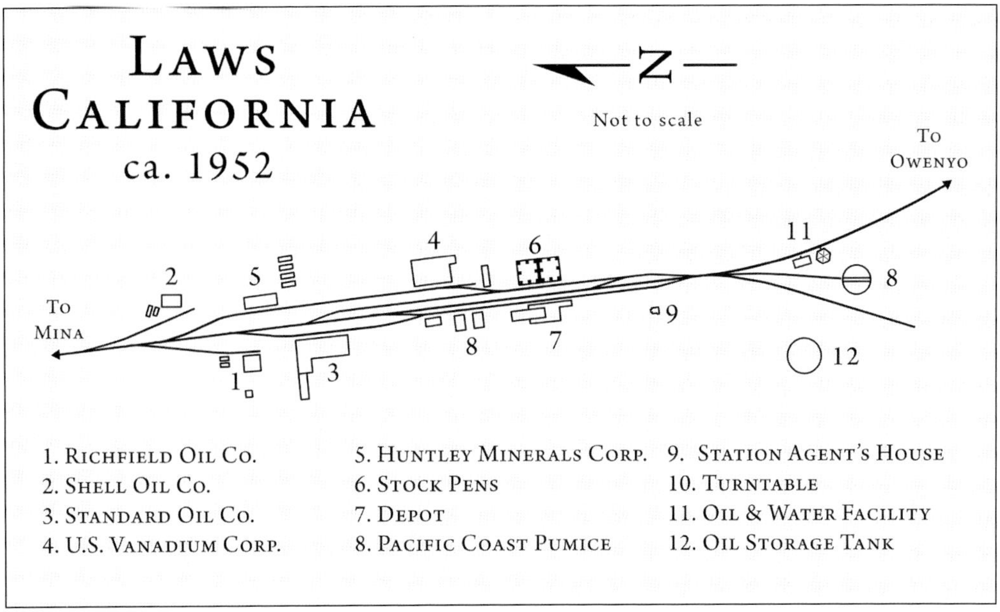

Laws served as the northern terminus of the railroad from 1942 until 1960. This map provides an overview of the many industries and railroad facilities located there in 1956.

An eastbound freight train enters the yard at Laws with the brakeman standing on the platform of caboose No. 467. No. 467 was built as SPC combine No. 63 in 1887. It was rebuilt into a caboose in 1908 and transferred to the N&C in 1909. In 1947, the caboose and two other cars were gifted to Parker W. Lyon's Pony Express Museum in Arcadia, California. In 1955, Lyon's museum was purchased by casino magnate William Harrah, who moved the collection to Sparks, Nevada, near his automobile museum. While stored in Nevada, No. 467 was nearly destroyed by fire in 1961. The remains were subsequently sold to several private owners. Today, the remains are privately owned, and some components have been used to restore C&C business car No. 2 and SP boxcar No. 54.

The southern end of the yard at Laws contained a turntable and oil and water tanks. Visible along the left side of this photograph is a 67,500-gallon oil tank used to store locomotive fuel. In the early 20th century, as the SP started converting locomotives to burn oil, it constructed numerous large-capacity storage tanks along its lines. The oil storage tank was removed in 1952.

Huntley Industrial Minerals constructed a substantial facility at Laws in 1932. Pyrophyllite mined in the White Mountains was brought to the company's grinding facility in Laws. The finished product was shipped in sacks to Owenyo and transferred to standard-gauge cars. The facility in Laws, seen here in 1952, outlasted the railroad by several years, finally ceasing operation in 1970. (Photograph by John Cummings; courtesy of the Herman Darr collection.)

Zurich was an important shipping point on the railroad. Blue Star Mining Company established a grinding facility at the start of World War II and processed tungsten during the war years. After the war, the facility was acquired by Huntley Industrial Materials, which produced 18 carloads of talc per week. The grinding mill burned down in 1950 and was not replaced, ending talc shipments from the station. (Photograph by John Cummings; courtesy of the Herman Darr collection.)

The depot at Zurich was constructed by the C&C in 1882 and originally named Alvord. In 1913, SP renamed the depot Zurich on account of the alpine scenery of the Sierra Nevada range to the west. A group of section houses for railroad employees can be seen on the left, along with a windmill used to pump water for residential use. (Courtesy of the Stephen E. Drew collection.)

Locomotive No. 18 passes over the trestle on the Owens River north of Tinemaha Reservoir. When the railroad was constructed during the 1880s, the main line kept to the eastern side of the river. Construction of the dam for the Tinemaha Reservoir necessitated realigning the main line to the west side of the river.

A freight train crosses Fish Slough as it heads south toward Owenyo. Fish Slough was located near Elna on the railroad. The trestle is still standing at the time of this publication and can be seen along Highway 395.

No. 9 and train passes through the cut on the new grade alignment on the western side of the Tinemaha Reservoir. The dam for the reservoir can be seen on the right-hand side of the image.

Locomotive No. 18 crosses the southern trestle over the Owens River as it heads eastbound toward Owenyo. The new alignment rejoined the original main line five miles north of Aberdeen. (Photograph by Fred Matthews; courtesy of the Stephen. E. Drew collection.)

The Keeler Branch was managed out of the Owenyo depot in later years. As Owenyo grew, the railroad outgrew the original boxcar depot and established a larger structure. William F. Tommer, the station agent, sits at his desk inside the Owenyo depot. Tommer went to work for the Southern Pacific Railroad in 1902. In 1924, he transferred to Owenyo and managed the railroad until he retired in 1954. He was well known throughout the Owens Valley, and locals often referred to the Slim Princess as "Mr. Tommer's Railroad."

The new Owenyo station building was constructed during the 1920s. The structure was constructed from two standard-gauge boxcar bodies with a common area in the middle under a single roof. After the railroad was scrapped in 1960, the building was moved to Keeler, where it is used by the volunteer fire department at the time of this writing.

This overall view of Owenyo from the north was taken from the roof of boxcars spotted at the end of the transfer platform track. The Owenyo Hotel, depot, and traveling gantry crane can be seen in the distance. Locomotive No. 8 and a water car sit on the service track to the left.

SP consolidation No. 2358 stands near the standard-gauge locomotive fuel tanks in Owenyo with an A-frame gondola in the foreground. Standard-gauge locomotives that operated over the Jawbone Branch to Owenyo were restricted to 10-wheelers (4-6-0), consolidation (2-8-0), and Mikado (2-8-2) types.

Locomotive No. 9 stands alongside SP standard-gauge RSD5 diesel No. 5297 in Owenyo in 1956. The antiquated narrow-gauge equipment retained the appearance of days gone by against the modern postwar world.

Locomotive No. 9 takes on water in Owenyo on the service track. On the opposite side of the yard, standing water and oil tanks were used to service standard-gauge locomotives. Water and oil pipelines crossed under the yard to the vertical "stand pipes" that served the narrow-gauge equipment.

The Owenyo traveling gantry crane was constructed for transferring electrical line poles from standard- to narrow-gauge cars during the 1910s. The crane remained in use until the end of the railroad in 1960.

Caboose No. 401 is loaded on a standard-gauge flatcar, having returned from SP's Los Angeles General Shops after an overhaul. Southern Pacific maintained a dedicated spur in Owenyo that allowed narrow-gauge equipment to be run up onto standard-gauge cars and shipped to Bakersfield for repair.

After the removal of the line between Mina and Benton, the narrow gauge was left without a shop complex to perform major work on locomotives. Each of the remaining locomotives on the line was shipped to Bakersfield for biannual servicing. Locomotive No. 9 has been loaded on a standard-gauge flatcar prior to shipment for repair.

General goods and sacked materials that traveled on the narrow gauge in boxcars had to be manually transferred to standard-gauge cars. At the Owenyo transfer platform, the contents of boxcar No. 66 are being transferred to standard-gauge SP boxcar No. 102856. It took two-and-a-half narrow-gauge cars to load a standard-gauge car to capacity.

The livestock transfer platform in Owenyo was built with a slight slope to facilitate the direct transfer of livestock. Narrow-gauge stock cars had lower decks, and the inclined platform eased transferring livestock into the taller standard-gauge cars.

Locomotive No. 18 switches in the Owenyo yard in preparation to move six loaded gondolas onto the transfer trestle (above). Strings of A-frame gondolas were pushed to the top of the transfer trestle, where they were dumped into standard-gauge cars waiting below (below).

Car repairs were performed at the Repair in Place (RIP) track at Owenyo. Tasks from residing to repainting equipment were performed here for freight and passenger cars as well as locomotives. Boxcar No. 130 is seen receiving new siding and repair work in 1952 (above). Caboose No. 401 receives new siding on the ends in addition to repairs of the draft gear and coupler in 1954 (below).

Locomotive No. 22 came to the SP from the Nevada-California-Oregon Railway but had an interesting life. No. 22 was built for the Florence & Cripple Creek Railroad (F&CC) of Colorado by the Schenectady Locomotive Works in 1899. When built, it carried the name "Vindicator" after one of the major mines in the Cripple Creek Mining region. The F&CC ceased operation in 1915 and sold No. 22 to the N-C-O. It later was transferred to SP's Mina Branch in 1928.

Locomotive No. 22 and business car No. 5 are seen heading south approaching Dolomite just north of Keeler. Business car No. 5 was built for the Denver South Park & Pacific Railroad of Colorado before being sold to the N-C-O in 1895. Like many pieces of N-C-O equipment, it was sent to the Mina Branch in 1928. As traffic dwindled over the narrow gauge, the use of business cars came to an end. In July 1940, business car No. 5 was converted to maintenance-of-way boarding car, and it was finally retired in 1944.

Locomotive No. 18 passes through Mount Whitney in 1956. After the depot was closed and removed, the yard at Mount Whitney was used to store equipment.

A freight train led by No. 9 passes the Dolomite spur. Dolomite was the northernmost of three spurs serving industries that worked a geologic structure comprised of marble, dolomite, and limestone. By the 1950s, these industries had closed but the sidings remained in use to store empty cars.

In 1948, a fan trip of railroad aficionados toured the narrow gauge. The train was led by locomotive No. 8 and paused in multiple locations along the line for photographs. Here, the train is stopped at Aberdeen, which, at this time, was little more than a water stop. A natural spring nearby supplied the tank and also created a lush landscape in what was otherwise a desert.

The October 7, 1948, fan trip sponsored by the Railway & Locomotive Historical Society leaves Owenyo for Laws. Railfans have attached a passenger car drumhead to the rear of caboose No. 401 bearing the name "Sage Brush Rocket."

The same October 7, 1948, fan trip pauses in Zurich. Railfans were treated to riding open cars on the trip, which were converted from gondolas and outfitted with primitive restroom accommodations. On the left side of the image is the substantial Blue Star Mining Company building.

The Mount Rubidoux Chapter of the Pacific Railroad Society sponsored a fan trip over the railroad on May 30, 1956. For the occasion, a passenger car drumhead was mounted on the rear of caboose No. 401 emblazoned with "Route of the Slim Princess." The train is stopped at Tinemaha cut for photographs.

The view looking north from the water tank at Keeler evokes memories of a long-gone time. This moody view presents the scenic beauty of the railroad in full display. The Sierra Nevada range looms in the distance, providing contrast with the desert climate of the Owens Valley below.

Five

End of the Line

With the removal of the line between Laws and Mina, what remained of the Slim Princess was a largely isolated freight railroad. The Keeler Branch primarily hauled bulk materials like tungsten, talc, dolomite, marble, perlite, and soda ash. Limited agricultural products continued to be shipped on the railroad, including seasonal livestock trains. World War II saw a slight increase in traffic over the railroad, as it hauled materials necessary to the war effort.

After the war, SP began cutting costs on narrow-gauge operations. Investments in equipment were curtailed, and the stable of narrow-gauge steam locomotives shrank. During the 1950s, SP reduced funding for maintaining equipment and facilities on the Keeler Branch. A diesel-electric locomotive was purchased in 1954 in an attempt to reduce the costs of maintaining steam locomotives, and the remaining three steam locomotives dwindled down to one held in reserve.

Despite these measures, the financial outlook of the railroad continued to decline, and the SP petitioned the Interstate Commerce Commission to abandon the line on January 20, 1960. After public meetings, the end came for the railroad on April 30, 1960, when the last revenue freight train was brought into Owenyo, ending nearly 80 years of operation. Scrapping soon followed, and a portion of the yard in Laws, including the turntable, depot, water and oil tanks, locomotive No. 9, a string of freight cars, and caboose No. 401, was donated to Inyo County.

In the fall of 1960, the L.B. Foster Company of Los Angeles was selected from a list of bidders to scrap the railroad. The four-mile stretch of standard-gauge track between Owenyo to Lone Pine was also removed. The railroad was only a memory when the company completed the job in early 1961. With the narrow gauge removed, the only standard-gauge portion of the former Carson & Colorado from Churchill to Mina remained. The 33-mile stretch from Thorne (near Hawthorne) to Mina was removed in 1991. At the time of this writing, the standard-gauge line from Churchill to Thorne is still in operation, serving the Hawthorne Army Depot.

The Bishop High School band performs for the crowd gathered to dedicate the Slim Princess's only diesel locomotive (above). Built by General Electric in 1954, the 50-ton locomotive was given the moniker "Little Giant" after a contest was held to give it a name. Railfans from Los Angeles took a weekend trip up to Owenyo to attend the event. Locomotive No. 18 was displayed alongside the Little Giant (below). Locomotive No. 9 handled two round-trip excursions between Owenyo and Keeler that day.

Locomotive No. 1, the Little Giant, awaits the next call in Owenyo in August 1956. It was built to a GE standard design, but the wheel sets were narrowed for use on the narrow gauge. This arrangement was intended to allow the locomotive to be converted to standard gauge in the event the narrow gauge was widened. After the railroad was scrapped in 1960, the locomotive spent its final days in Mexico and was finally scrapped in 2018. (Courtesy of the Stephen E. Drew collection.)

With the age of the steam locomotive drawing to a close, nostalgia in the form of fan trips and special displays paid tribute to the fading technology. Sometimes that nostalgia was misguided, as was the case with this paint scheme applied to No. 9. In 1956, the Bakersfield shop took it upon themselves to dress up a locomotive of their own and painted No. 9 in a shocking scheme of black with red and gold accents complete with a fake box headlamp and diamond stack. The narrow-gauge crews were not pleased to find the locomotive dressed up in this fashion and returned the locomotive to a much more normal scheme within a year.

The open-air engine facility in Keeler grew out of necessity after the enginehouse fire in 1946. Tank car No. 353 was stationed on a short stretch of track to supply fuel to locomotives. A small lean-to structure was constructed, giving the workers shade from the harsh desert climate. Locomotive Nos. 8 and 9 can be seen on the drop pit track in the distance.

Locomotive No. 8 passes the water tank as it enters the yard at Keeler from the north. The tank at Keeler was oriented for locomotives on the main line to take on water.

Several industries were located on the southern end of Keeler. The Sierra Talc Company is seen on the right. On the left is the Cerro Gordo Tramway terminal building. After the tramway ceased operation, the spur was used to store empty or bad order cars awaiting repair.

The Keeler depot was constructed as a smaller structure in 1883. By 1920, the structure had been expanded and remodeled into the building seen here. The original freight building was joined to newer construction and living quarters for the agent. Around 1956, visiting railroad fans installed the "Carson & Colorado Railway" sign on the roof in honor of the railroad's history. The depot closed in August 1957, and station agent George Wood was transferred to Lone Pine.

The American Perlite Company operated a mine north of the railroad near Elna. Perlite is an amorphous (non-crystalline) form of obsidian with high water content. To transport the material, the company constructed a loading facility at the siding at Elna in 1958. Perlite has several industrial uses, with the largest being an additive to potting soil. (Both photographs by Lee Klaus; courtesy of Herman Darr.)

After the Blue Star Grinding plant burned down in 1950, Zurich generated minimal freight traffic. The depot, which had been closed since 1932, was torn down in 1955. What little remained was removed with the railroad. Concrete building foundations from the former industries still remain at the site of Zurich.

Steam locomotive No. 9 handles the duty of pushing the Little Giant onto a flatcar for shipment to Bakersfield for maintenance. No. 9 was the last steam locomotive to operate on the railroad and was kept on standby during the final years. This scene from 1959 is one of the last runs No. 9 made before the railroad was scrapped. (Courtesy of the Martin E. Hansen collection.)

Locomotive No. 8 is seen on the siding at Walong riding a standard-gauge flatcar over the famed Tehachapi Loop in October 1953. The locomotive is being returned to Owens Valley after servicing in Bakersfield (above). With the arrival of the Little Giant, No. 8 was deemed excess and donated to the state of Nevada. It was displayed for many years at Boswell's Eagle Territory Museum in Carson City (below) before being moved to Sparks for display. (Both, courtesy of the Stephen E. Drew collection.)

The Little Giant approaches Kearsarge with a loaded train en route to Owenyo (above). The Kearsarge depot was formerly located on the right-hand side of the image below. At the time of this photograph, the passing siding, section houses, and water tank were all that remained.

April 4, 1960, was the last day of revenue service on the railroad. The Little Giant is seen with engineer Walter "Fergie" Ferguson standing on the end platform and fireman Graves standing down below. On April 30, the railroad was officially abandoned and sold for scrap.

The Little Giant waits in Owenyo for the scrappers to take over the railroad in 1960. After the scrapping job was completed, Little Giant was converted to standard gauge and used by the SP. It was later sold to the Cananea Copper Mining Company in Mexico. By 2004, it was out of service but stored at the mine for many years. It was finally scrapped in 2018.

Railroad historian Richard Datin photographed the scrapping efforts on the railroad in late 1960. At Kearsarge, he found gondolas Nos. 203 and 205 removed from the track in partial states of scrapping. Gondola No. 205 is flipped over on the right-hand side of the track. On the left side is gondola No. 202, which was simply shoved off the track nearly into one of the abandoned bunkhouses.

Gondola No. 323 and stock car Nos. 159 and 167 are among the cars gathered by the scrapper in Zurich. The two stock cars escaped the scrapper's torch, becoming part of the collection acquired by William Harrah. No. 159 was built for the SPC as flatcar No. 835 in 1890 while stock car No. 173 was constructed on former C&C flatcar No. 72. In 1988, both cars were sold to the Nevada State Railroad Museum, and in 2017, stock car No. 173 was converted back into a flatcar and restored to its original C&C number.

Boxcars No. 20 and No. 12 were among the last pieces of equipment to move over the line. The two cars are seen in Zurich during the scrapping of the railroad. These cars were part of a group sold to William Harrah for display at his automobile museum in Sparks, Nevada. Visible on the cars is the logo of Harrah's casino. Harrah's sold the cars in 1988 to Gary Norwood for use on his railroad at the Silverwood Theme Park in Athol, Idaho. In 2020, the cars were acquired by the Sumpter Valley Railroad in Oregon where they await restoration.

Scrapping materials and equipment were brought to Owenyo and scrapped there. Richard Datin visited Owenyo in the fall of 1960 and photographed this scene. The lower transfer platform and perlite loader can be seen standing above the debris in the yard. In a few short months, the structures and facilities were completely removed.

Scrapping of the railroad is in full swing at Owenyo. Most of the railroad structures have been removed, including the depot and the Owenyo hotel. The remains of several cars can be seen in the foreground.

These photographs show the remains left behind shortly after the railroad was removed from Keeler. Many railroad-related structures, including the depot, tool houses, and water tank, were left in place. Many of these structures remain in place at the time of writing, making Keeler a unique time capsule of days gone by. The water tank from Keeler is now at the Southern California Railway Museum for restoration.

After the railroad was removed, the ties and grade were left in place. In this scene of the grade south of Owenyo, the abandoned line stretches into the horizon.

Mina remained an active shipping point long after the narrow gauge was removed. In this photograph taken in 1967, former C&C caboose coach No. 1 stands in the former "Car Town." Two F7 diesel locomotives sit idle on the main line in the background awaiting their next assignment. Caboose coach No. 1 was acquired by Richard Datin and donated to the Laws Railroad Museum, where it awaits restoration.

Despite being four miles from Lone Pine, Owenyo was home to many railroad employees who lived in small houses clustered around the standard-gauge wye. The southern end of the wye can be seen in this view, and the pump house for the water tank is visible at left. On the right are employee houses built after 1916.

SP No. 1 and gondola No. 204 are seen in Zurich during scrapping operations in late 1960. Gondola No. 204 survived the railroad, being sold to the Midwest Central Railroad in Mount Pleasant, Iowa. The car was converted into a passenger car for hauling tourists with the addition of a body riding atop the car frame. Original paint and lettering from the end of the SP are still visible underneath.

Six

Rolling Stock

No history of the Slim Princess would be complete without a discussion of the equipment used on the line. The C&C's initial rolling stock was built largely at the Virginia & Truckee Railroad shops in Carson City, Nevada. In the years following the SP's purchase of the C&C, the original rolling stock was replaced by equipment transferred from SP's other narrow-gauge lines during the Tonopah boom. Equipment from the South Pacific Coast Railroad (some of which started life on the Oregonian Railway) and the San Joaquin & Sierra Nevada Railroad was leased or transferred to the C&C.

Equipment remaining from the Tonopah boom was replaced or rebuilt thoroughly. Work that was too heavy for the facilities in Mina was sent via standard-gauge car to Sparks, where the SP maintained a massive shop complex. When required, new cars were constructed or modified. In 1917, when the aging fleet of flatcars and gondolas began to wear out, 50 new cars were built in the shops at Sparks, Nevada, and Ogden, Utah.

In 1925, the Southern Pacific leased the Lake Tahoe Railway & Transportation Co. and converted it to standard gauge a year later. Eight boxcars, some of which started life on the Tonopah Railroad, were moved to Mina and remained in service until the end of the line. SP acquired the Nevada–California–Oregon Railway in April of the same year. The N-C-O was a substantial railroad in its own right that operated along the eastern Sierra Nevada range from Reno to Alturas. During the conversion from narrow to standard gauge, a large amount of equipment was sent to Mina, replacing the aging cars previously brought over during the Tonopah boom.

Today, 3 locomotives and 64 pieces of rolling stock are preserved in 13 railroad museums and tourist railroads across the country. When the railroad was scrapped in 1960, many car bodies were sold locally, some of which remain in Owens Valley and are used as sheds and outbuildings. Volunteers of the nonprofit Carson & Colorado Railway completed the restoration of locomotive No. 18 to service in 2017. Since restoration, No. 18 has operated in Laws on original SP rails as well as in Nevada and Colorado.

Derrick car No. 1 was built in the 1880s for the Central Pacific Railroad. In 1900, the car was renumbered SP 636; soon afterward, it was converted to narrow gauge and renumbered derrick car No. 1. At 36 feet long and 9 feet 6 inches wide, the car would not fit through the tunnel on Montgomery Pass. When the line from Mina to Benton was abandoned, the car was not transferred to the Owens Valley.

A wrecking outfit is pictured alongside the Mina enginehouse. The support train for derrick No. 1 consisted of five cars given the number 1 and an alphabetical suffix. 1A was a wheel and tie car used as the derrick's tender. 1B was former caboose No. 1009 and later became caboose No. 401. 1C started life as a boxcar converted to tool service. 1D was a caboose from the SPC used as a bunk car.

Baggage car No. 12 served the railroad until 1960 when it was donated to Travel Town, a railroad museum established in Los Angeles's Griffith Park. It was built by the Carter Brothers Builders in Newark, California, for the Oregonian Railway of Oregon in 1880. After the SP acquired the Oregonian, it was sent to the SPC, where it was converted into a baggage and railway post office car and transferred to the C&C during the Tonopah boom. In 1927, it was rebuilt into a full baggage car. After passenger service was discontinued, the car was used as a caboose.

SP 1010 began life on the San Joaquin & Sierra Nevada Railroad, built by its shops in Lodi in 1882. After the SP acquired the SJ&SN, it transferred the car to the South Pacific Coast Railroad. In 1904, it was sent to the C&C for use during the Tonopah boom. It was used into the N&C era until December 1913 when the car was retired; the body was used to house employees in the Car Town area of Mina. It was restored by the Society for the Preservation of Carter Railroad Resources (SPCRR) at the Ardenwood living history preserve in Fremont, California. (Photograph by Randy Hees.)

The Southern Pacific modified 10 boxcars to haul perlite from Elna to the transfer at Owenyo. These modifications included building A-frame sloped sheets inside the car and the addition of hatches on the roof and sides of the car, effectively making them covered hopper cars. Perlite was loaded through the top hatches for shipment to Owenyo. Upon arrival, the cars were unloaded through the lower hatches into a loading conveyor at the southern end of the transfer platform into standard-gauge cars. Perlite car No. 73 was sold after the railroad was scrapped. It was acquired by the Southern Pacific Narrow Gauge Historical Society and is undergoing restoration at the Eastern California Museum in Independence, California.

Stock car No. 65 was built in 1912 by the Nevada–California–Oregon Railway as stock car No. 159. After Southern Pacific acquired the N-C-O, many pieces of equipment from the N-C-O were sent to the Mina Branch to replace older, worn-out equipment. Former N-C-O stock car No. 159 became SP 173 in 1929 and was renumbered to 65 in 1946. Tropico Gold Mine acquired the car in 1960. It was later donated to the Southern California Narrow Gauge Museum, where it is preserved today.

Four flatcars were rebuilt for hauling sugar beets in the 1920s. Sugar Beet traffic on the narrow gauge was short-lived, and the cars were put into service hauling coke by the 1930s. During the final years of the railroad, the cars were repurposed as livestock cars for hauling sheep.

Gondola No. 225 is captured in Owenyo with the full beauty of the Sierra Nevada range and Mount Whitney (center of image) looming over the scene. It was built as a flatcar by the SP shops in Ogden, Utah, in 1917. It was sold to William Harrah in 1960 and later to the Silverwood Theme Park in Athol, Idaho, where it was rebuilt into a passenger car for the park's tourist railroad.

Flat-bottom gondolas like No. 202 were lined with sheet metal to prevent the loose material transported in them from shaking through boards in transit. Many cars had a single removable portion on one side, allowing material to be loaded with the aid of trucks or small front-end loaders. When the cars reached Owenyo, the material needed to be unloaded at one of the transfer platforms manually. Material shipped in gondolas of this type was typically large.

Gondola No. 310 was built for the South Pacific Coast Railroad in 1885. In 1917, it was rebuilt as an A-frame gondola for shipping bulk material to Owenyo. A-frame gondolas were capable of discharging their load through the side doors using gravity. When positioned on the transfer trestle at Owenyo, the load could be emptied into the standard-gauge cars below.

A-frame gondolas had several variations, including four or five side doors. Some cars had standing vertical posts to reinforce the A-frame structure that protruded through the A-frame, and others did not, as demonstrated in this photograph showing the interior of No. 310 in the foreground and an unidentified car behind it.

SP boxcar No. 26 started life on the Florence & Cripple Creek Railroad of Colorado. Built in 1899 by the St. Charles Car Company of St. Charles, Missouri, and originally numbered 567, it was among a group of cars sold by the F&CC to the N-C-O in 1915. When the SP changed the N-C-O 15 to standard gauge, boxcars of this type were moved to the Mina Branch. No. 26 was sold to Universal Studios in 1955. In 1985, it was loaned to the Nevada County Historical Society and moved to Nevada City, California. From 2000 to 2002, it was restored and is now on display at the Nevada County Narrow Gauge Railroad Museum in Nevada City, California.

Boxcar No. 130 started life on the Tonopah Railroad in 1904. After the Tonopah Railroad conversion to standard gauge, it was one of four cars sold to the Lake Tahoe Railway & Transportation Company (LTR&T) and served the line until 1925, when the SP purchased the railroad. After the LTR&T was converted to standard gauge, it was sent to the Mina Branch. When the railroad was scrapped, the body was sold to a local ranch, where it remained until 2009, when it was acquired by the Nevada County Narrow Gauge Railroad Museum.

Boxcars No. 7 and No. 132 were sold to railfan Cal Rogers in 1959. The two cars were used on a fan trip in 1956 where Rogers re-lettered boxcar No. 7 for the Carson & Colorado. Boxcar No. 7 started life as South Pacific Coast Railroad boxcar No. 66, built by Carter Brothers Builders in the 1880s. It was transferred to the N&C in 1907 as boxcar No. 414. During the 1946–1947 renumbering, it became boxcar No. 7. In 1960, the two cars were donated to Inyo County for display at Laws.

Combination passenger car No. 8 started life as South Pacific Coast Railway coach no. 60, built by Harlan & Hollingsworth Car Builders in Wilmington, Delaware, in 1889. In 1907, the car was sent to the Mina Branch, becoming N&C coach No. 9. As passenger service wound down on the railroad, it was converted to combination passenger car No. 8. It was sold to Parker Lyon for display at his Pony Express Museum. In 1955, William Harrah acquired Lyon's collection, and No. 8 was moved to Sparks, Nevada. In 1986, Gary Norton purchased the car at auction for his Silverwood Theme Park in Idaho. In 1991, the car was purchased by the Nevada State Railroad Museum in Carson City, where it awaits restoration.

Gasoline and oil were transported on the railroad during the first quarter of the 20th century. Oil and gasoline were hauled on the narrow gauge to several bulk oil distributors at Zurich and Laws. Competition from trucks and improved roads siphoned the oil business away, and shipment by rail declined in the 1930s. Ten tank cars were sold to the US Navy in 1942 for use at the Pearl Harbor Naval Supply Depot. The SP shops in Sacramento built tank car No. 174 during the mid-1920s. It was off the roster by 1943, possibly among the cars transferred to the Navy.

Tank car No. 352 was stored at Owenyo in the final years of the railroad. In 1960, it was donated to the Railway & Locomotive Historical Society and later gifted to the State of California for the California State Railroad Museum. It was restored in 1979 to its pre-1947 appearance as No. 145. It is displayed on the second floor of the museum with other narrow-gauge equipment, including SP boxcar No. 46.

In 1948, flatcar No. 209 was sent to Bakersfield as the pilot in a program to upgrade the aging wooden cars with steel components. The trucks and other hardware were retained while a new body frame was constructed of steel. This program was canceled immediately, and further improvements to the narrow gauge were curtailed. (Photograph by John Cummings; courtesy of the Herman Darr collection.)

A-frame gondola No. 333 was built by the N-C-O as a flatcar and converted to a gondola by the SP. After operations on the Keeler Branch ceased, it was among a group of cars sold to the Roaring Camp Big Trees & Pacific. The hardware from these cars was used to build the narrow-gauge passenger cars still used by the railroad today. (Courtesy of the Stephen E. Drew collection.)

Flatcar No. 200 was a survivor of the original Carson & Colorado equipment built by the V&T shops in Carson City. Here, it is parked on the turntable spur where old equipment was stored. The original C&C lettering showing the car number 8 can be seen near the middle of the car. Soon after this photograph was taken, the car was scrapped. (Photograph by John Cummings; courtesy of the Herman Darr collection.)

Like a scene from days gone by, the recently restored locomotive No. 18 glides through the yard in Laws on October 24, 2017. After several years of hard work by the volunteers of the Carson & Colorado Railway, No. 18 was restored to operation in 2017. Volunteers of the Bishop County Historical Society worked for many years to relay the track removed from Laws in 1960. The dedication of both groups is bringing the Slim Princess back to life nearly 80 years after the railroad was removed.

Bibliography

Bader, Robert A. *Southern Pacific Narrow Gauge Locomotives and Freight Equipment*. Pasadena, CA: Southern Pacific Historical Technical Society, 2011.

Bender, Henry E. Jr. *Southern Pacific Lines Standard-Design Depots*. Berkeley and Wilton, CA: Signature Press, 2013.

Datin, Richard C. Jr. "The Carson & Colorado RR. Eastern California Museum, Independence, CA." Unpublished manuscript.

Enss, Chris. *A Beautiful Mine: Women Prospectors of the Old West*. Guilford, CT: TwoDot, 2008.

Ferrell, Mallory Hope. *Southern Pacific Narrow Gauge*. Edmonds, WA: Pacific Fast Mail, 1982.

Gotchy, L.T. *From Keeler to Laws*. San Bernardino, CA: Writer's Lair, 2017.

Morris, Joe Dale. *Southern Pacific's Slim Princess in the Sunset*. Pasadena, CA: Southern Pacific Historical Technical Society, 2008.

Myles, Myrtle T. "Jim Butler: Nevada's Improbable Tycoon" *Montana: The Magazine of Western History* Vol. 26, No. 1 (Winter, 1976) 60-69.

Myrick, *David F. Railroads of Nevada & Eastern California Vol. 1*. Reno, NV: University of Nevada Press, 1992.

———. *Railroads of Nevada & Eastern California Vol. 3*. Reno, NV: University of Nevada Press, 2007.

Serpico, Philip C. *Jawbone: Sunset on the Lone Pine*. Palmdale, CA: Omni Publications, 2006.

———. *Tonopah & Tidewater: The Nevada Short Line*. Palmdale, CA: Omni Publications, 2013.

Shamberger, Hugh A. *Candelaria and Its Neighbors*. Carson City, NV: Nevada Historical Press, 1978.

Silver, Sue. *Mineral County Nevada Vol. 3*. Hawthorne, NV: Museum Association of Mineral County, 2011.

Turner, George. *Slim Rails Through the Sand: The Saga of the Carson & Colorado-Southern Pacific Narrow-gauge Railroad Through the Desert*. Glendale, CA: Trans-Anglo Books, 1989.